To Shelagh,
Love Mummy

May, 2013

WELCOME TO YOUR NEW LIFE

WELCOME TO YOUR NEW LIFE

anna goldsworthy

Black Inc.

Published by Black Inc.,
an imprint of Schwartz Media Pty Ltd
37–39 Langridge Street
Collingwood VIC 3066 Australia
email: enquiries@blackincbooks.com
http://www.blackincbooks.com

Copyright © Anna Goldsworthy 2013

ALL RIGHTS RESERVED.
No part of this publication may be reproduced, stored in a retrieval system, or transmitted in any form by any means electronic, mechanical, photocopying, recording or otherwise without the prior consent of the publishers.

National Library of Australia Cataloguing-in-Publication entry

Goldsworthy, Anna.

Welcome to your new life / Anna Goldsworthy.

9781863955935 (pbk.)

Goldsworthy, Anna. Pregnant women – Biography. First pregnancy.

920.72

Book design by Peter Long
Typeset by Duncan Blachford

Printed in Australia by Griffin Press. The paper this book is printed on is certified against the Forest Stewardship Council® Standards. Griffin Press holds FSC chain of custody certification SGS-COC-005088. FSC promotes environmentally responsible, socially beneficial and economically viable management of the world's forests.

WELCOME

YOU

At first the idea amuses me. I do not even recognise it as my own. It has been sixteen years since I have eaten meat and I have seldom missed it. But this hits with the specificity of a crush. I do not just crave any old sausage, I crave *this* sausage: a stocky turd-like *cevapi*. Years of abstinence vanish, as my mouth remembers, my tongue remembers. The sausage's loud clang against the tastebuds, of spice and flesh and fat. Its dissolution in the mouth: a little rank, a little corrupt. The communion of it, against my tongue, in my body. And how I feel afterwards. Fed. Replete.

If a vegetarian eats a sausage and no-one is there to see it, is it still meat?

Over the days that follow, the craving becomes overwhelming. My body hums with it until I am afraid others can hear it too. At the musical competition I am adjudicating, I strain to hear the children play. Finally I make a decision. I dart over to the shops at morning tea and return with a discreet white paper bag.

And now that I have it I might as well use it, rather than ruin the day with suspense.

When I return to the auditorium, the volunteers are drinking the same milky tea. The students are lined up in the same uniforms; their mothers offer the same hopeful smiles. The *cevapi* settles into a vindicated silence, so that I am better able to hear the students play. Even the worst performances have a strange beauty. My pen keeps moving, as I tell them to sing more, to trust themselves, to listen to the sounds they make. A tiny Japanese girl flees the stage; a child catches my eye as he bows. And all the while I smile at you, in secret. You are the best type of private joke.

LIFE

'Why the spontaneous dinner plans?' asks Nicholas, as we pull up at the red light.

I switch on the wipers to distract him, but there is not enough rain and they blur loudly across the windscreen. 'You'll find out.'

He turns to me suspiciously. 'You're not pregnant, are you?'

It is not the way I would have scripted it, but it will have to do.

At the restaurant, he is silent through main course, laughs uproariously during dessert, and then is silent again. Only when the waiter clears away our plates does he speak.

'I hope we're doing the right thing by it.'

'What?'

'Making it alive.'

Three months ago I was in a car accident in Germany. It was a high speed head-on collision and it seemed unlikely we should have survived. I had been dozing in the back seat alongside the other members of my trio, and was awoken by a collective intake of breath. And then that infinite moment – the wonder, the surrender, the terrible patience of it – as the noise and the pain moved through my body, and I waited to see if I was still alive.

Afterwards we lay on the frozen road, gasping for breath, while bystanders gathered around us.

'Are you really from Australia? You have these – how do you say – *kangaroos* in Australia, yes?'

'And these little bears. What is it that you call them? Koalas.'

I had sprained some ribs, fractured my spine in three places, dislodged a splinter of bone that now floated around my vertebral column. That night, I struggled to remember how to breathe. And at the same time, I could not sleep for outrage. For the rude reminder: *there is no safety*. Above all, I wanted Nicholas's arms around me, but instead I took out my iPod and listened to Fritz Wunderlich singing Schumann. His honeyed voice was another form of embrace, affirming the laws of inhalation and exhalation, alongside those other laws of beauty and order – illusory laws, perhaps, but ones I needed to believe in – until the black room lightened to grey and I could get up.

Back home in Melbourne, I still cannot sleep. There is a place deep within my chest that bore the brunt of the insult; each night my muscles contract around it, as if bracing again for impact. Nicholas buys me a robotic massage chair, and I sit on it as he sleeps, waiting for my body to forget, to relax its vigilance.

Tonight, while the chair kneads my back, I cast an objective eye over life, as one might reappraise a Christmas gift before giving. There might be no safety, but there is love and curiosity. Denial, lotteries, porridge and video. Mozart and hydrangeas. Blood and milk. Wormholes and composting toilets. (It is a long list if you do it properly.) Sleep, outings, snakes, words. Childhood all over again. Having to tell you about your own death. Hoping to subject you to my own, one day.

After some time, the contractions subside, and I return to bed.

'I think it is the right thing,' I venture. 'All things considered.'

Nicholas turns. 'What?'

'Life.'

He throws a subduing arm around me and the conversation is over.

In the morning I call your Grandmother Baba, and there is a whoosh of bath water as she takes in the news. 'You cheeky little devil!' Then her voice becomes crisp, medical. 'How many days are you overdue? Have you booked an obstetrician?'

Your Pop does not answer his phone, so I try your Aunt Sash instead: '*Fuck off!*'

'It's going to take us all a long time to get used to this,' your Uncle Daniel says sternly, from London.

'Happy days!' exclaims Great-Grandma Moggy. 'But how on earth will you manage, darling?'

'That's great news!' says Pop, when he finally answers his phone. 'Or is it?'

'I think so. Yes.'

'It's going to be disruptive.'

'Yes, but how much more disruptive for this former non-entity!' Unfortunately for my father, I am armed with the reflections of a sleepless night. 'Detaching itself from nothingness! Beginning its valiant, lonely trek to selfhood!'

'That's a good point.'

'We spend all this time pondering death, but Dad, death is nothing, it's just the return to default. This is the amazing bit: *the reverse of death is occurring in my belly*. Of all the world's locations!'

I hear the faint percussion of typing.

'Are you working?'

'Sorry, sweetie, just had to send an email.' He clears his throat, channelling a medical authority of his own. 'Let me just say one thing. If your body's telling you to eat a sausage, then *eat the damn sausage.*'

But now that the sausage has fulfilled its purpose, it has retreated. We set off to find a doctor, who administers a second test and refers us to the ultrasound clinic, where a young sonographer rubs gel on my stomach and applies the humming transducer. Her movements are business-like and efficient, as if this is nothing out of the ordinary, as if she reveals new life to parents all the time.

'You're quite far along. Possibly about ten weeks. Would you like to see?'

And there you are, a frantic beating inch. Obscured by my tears, you are blurry as a distant galaxy, except for the insistent flashing of your heart. I feel such tenderness for that heartbeat, for its certainty, its dogged commitment to life. It is the good that trumps everything.

That's great news. Yes, it is.

DENIAL

At ten weeks, you are no longer embryo but foetus. You are a small strawberry, with nipples. I carry your polaroid in my wallet, admiring you throughout the day. Your stowaway cunning amuses me: the way you concealed yourself as embryo, coming out only when foetus.

There are advantages to being out of touch with my body: I have made it to the end of the first trimester without noticing morning sickness. There are disadvantages, too. Every obstetrician we call has been booked up for weeks by women more self-aware.

I mention this to a neighbour's new girlfriend, a student of midwifery. 'You don't need an *obstetrician*.' She spits out the word like an expletive. Her soft face is covered with down, fine as lanugo.

'Why not?'

'The medicalisation of childbirth is about the *pathologisation of the female*. Studies show that male doctors repeatedly engage in excessive penetrations during labour.'

'What sort of penetrations?'

Her tiny rosebud mouth twists to one side. 'Digital rape, for one thing.'

I visit my friend Fiona, who has recently given birth using an obstetrician. She is practising cello in the kitchen while her infant daughter sleeps in a bassinet beside her, compliant as a household appliance.

'Did you feel digitally raped during childbirth?' I ask.

'God, no. I felt *empowered*!' She returns the cello to its case and fills up the kettle. 'Giving birth was the greatest physical triumph of my life.'

The baby wakes herself with a large grunt, and Fiona buries her nose in her nappy. 'Heaven!' She offers the child's bottom to me. 'Please. Have a whiff. It's the most *delicious* bacon-and-egg croissant.'

I sniff delicately. 'It's certainly tangy.'

'Have you written your birth plan?' she asks, as she places the baby on the kitchen bench and changes her.

'Birth plan?'

'You know. The script of your labour, your delivery. Pain relief, but other things too. Preferred positions. Choice of music.' She takes a DVD from a shelf. 'You won't believe this, but Matilda crowned exactly at the recapitulation of the Elgar concerto!'

I catch a glimpse of the DVD's title before it is swallowed into the machine: *Matilda's birth. December 14.*

'I do believe it. I don't need video evidence.'

'But I'd like to share this with you.'

Is it bad manners to decline a childbirth video with your tea?

Panic rises in me like nausea. Then I realise it is nausea and run to the bathroom, embracing morning sickness like deliverance. When I return, the DVD has been removed, and Fiona has brewed a pot of ginger tea.

'I think you're in denial. When you're ready, you should watch my video. Or if for some reason you don't want to watch mine, you should at least watch somebody else's.'

'It's not that I don't want to watch yours in particular. If I was going to watch anyone's, it would definitely be yours.'

She waves her hand impatiently. 'Preparation is *key*. Think of labour as the biggest performance of your life. I swam two kilometres a day when I was pregnant, but that was the least of it. It's all about *psychological* preparation.'

The baby hiccups politely, and Fiona attaches her to a neat breast.

'What sort of psychological preparation?'

'YouTube is a great resource. I watched all sorts of animals being born. Chimpanzees, hippos, baby whales. And I watched other things, too.'

As the child drinks, she makes the noise of an outboard motor. It is extravagant, orgasmic, a celebration of appetite.

A pink flush creeps up Fiona's neck. 'I wish she wouldn't do that.'

The baby's tiny mouth works up and down, and the hooligan noises grow louder. I marvel at how she can drink and yell at once: surely it requires circular breathing.

'What other things?'

She places a hand over her yodelling baby's ear and drops her voice. 'Porn.'

'Why?'

'To overcome my squeamishness.'

'What sort of porn?'

'Insertion of objects. Fisting. Anything that challenged me.' She moves the child from one breast to the other and tucks away the depleted nipple. 'There's a lot of weird stuff out there, if you make the effort to find it.'

I already have a lurid conception of childbirth, furnished by Baba and Sash. Baba's near-fatal haemorrhaging when I was born, because of a family bleeding disorder; Sash's regular dispatches from the frontline, during her years of medical training. Of a labouring woman defecating into her hand, hurling her faeces against the hospital walls. 'We came running in to find a shit storm, literally. Flying here, flying there! The nurses huddled in the corner, screaming.'

Into this surreal landscape, I now have to introduce digital rape, alongside the helpfulness of fisting. As I drive home, I glance down and am reassured by your size. Labour is still a long way away, still largely hypothetical. Some supremely improbable events have to occur first. I have to grow an extra brain inside my belly, a spare pair of ears.

When I arrive home, Nicholas is on the phone. He hangs up and then sits on the sofa beside me, cradling my hand.

'That was Fiona. Do you think you might be in labour denial?'

*

At twelve weeks, you have grown fingernails and a pancreas. Pain has been switched on. Sometimes you cry silently in the womb, but what do you have to cry about, little bean? Are you lonely in there, with your unseen, unknown face?

I am determined not to be in denial, so I begin swotting pregnancy books. Preparing for birth, it seems, is like preparing for a wedding. There are guests to invite, soundtracks to organise, catering to plan.

Spare a thought for your husband who will doubtless become peckish as you labour. You may not have time to bake once labour begins, so why not prepare in advance? It can be a good idea to bake muffins beforehand and freeze. Start to defrost when you feel those early, mild contractions.

'Why do you find that so amusing?' asks Nicholas, as I read this to him in bed.

Now that I am aware of them, birth plans are everywhere. My email inbox brims with their successful realisations.

Surrounded by a nurturing circle of love, Archie was born joyfully into water.

After a second entirely drug-free labour, Laila has arrived to join Mummy, Daddy and Big Sis Cecilia.

There is a stridency to them that I had not previously noticed, and I begin to dread their arrival, feeling reprimanded in advance for a drug-assisted labour that has not yet taken place. I confess this to Grace and Bruno, who have been attending hypnosis classes in preparation for a drug-free birth.

'No-one's judging you,' Bruno says. 'The issue is more society's expectations around birth pain.'

Grace's pregnancy is four months more advanced than my own, a reassuring buttress between me and labour. She is glowing, as pregnant women are supposed to, and wears her hair wrapped in a dramatic red turban. 'We have the most wonderful *doula*. She's going to coach us through the entire birth experience, even the pain.'

Bruno takes her hand. 'But there will be no pain, my *cocotte*. We have learnt this already in the classes. Labour pain is *completely* a social construct.'

This is something I would like to believe. 'Really?'

'*Absolutely*. If you go in without the expectation of pain, you simply will not feel any. This is the point of the hypnosis.'

'Birth can be a really sensuous experience,' Grace explains. When she is anxious she smiles widely, and now her perfect teeth gleam at me. 'Apparently, some women have the most powerful orgasms of their life when they give birth. I'm not necessarily aiming for one. An orgasm would just be a bonus.'

I have never heard of a doula, but immediately I want one: barefoot, enlightened, smelling of lavender oil. A script forms in my imagination, of candles, ambient music, the soothing ministrations of a doula. A midwife catching you, possibly into joyful water. A small happy splash, and then a baby's tinkling laughter. A group hug. Maybe even a singalong.

I admit this fantasy to Sash over the phone. Foolishly, I use the expression *birth experience*.

'Oh yes, we all love *experiences*,' she begins. 'Candles, essential oils, warm water. Aren't they lovely? Go on, have an *experience*. You work hard, you deserve it! Run yourself a warm bath. Listen to some Enya.'

'I wasn't planning to listen to Enya.'

'But guess what? Sometimes things go wrong in childbirth. And when they go wrong, they go *very* wrong. Here's an idea: have your experience when you're *not* having a baby!'

I can never manage a rebuttal when under attack from my sister.

'Why would anyone risk their child's life *for an experience*? And in your case especially. You've got a fractured back. A bleeding disorder!'

Suddenly I find my rebuttal. 'Studies show that male doctors repeatedly engage in excessive penetrations during labour.'

'Like what?'

My voice falters. 'You know. Digital rape.'

There is an ominous silence.

'Do you even understand what giving birth is? It is a *reverse penetration*! The biggest one you're ever going to have. If you feel violated by a doctor's pinkie, how do you plan to cope with your baby's *enormous head*?'

'That's a good point.'

'Run yourself a bath and meditate on it for a while.'

After I hang up, I do just that. And as the bath fills around me, I come to a decision: the size of a baby's head is a feminist issue. It is poor design that our heads are too big for our pelvises, but why should women be the ones to pay? Should we not use our expanded brain capacity – the source of the pain – to ease our torment? Instead, we demand stoicism. Orgasms. Muffins. And then we email our masochistic triumphs to everyone in our address book.

I start a new birth plan by finding an obstetrician. Monica has a clear scrubbed face and the trim body of an athlete. Her form-fitting pencil skirt refutes all my chaotic notions of childbirth. I tell her about my fractured spine, my bleeding disorder. A tiny furrow, needle-thin, bisects her brow. 'You're an interesting patient. It's good to have interesting patients.'

Then she takes my blood pressure, and asks me to lie down. She applies a doppler stethoscope to my stomach so that I can eavesdrop on your heartbeat, blessed and improbable as life on Mars.

LOTTERY

At thirteen weeks, you have developed the rooting reflex, swivelling your empty mouth towards movement, as if movement itself might feed you. Your larynx and vocal cords are already finished, but your voice will remain secret for another six months, even to you.

'What do you feel towards your unborn child?' Grace asks.

'A type of love, I suppose.'

She regards my bump with alarmed eyes, as if it is the victim of neglect. 'Why only a type of love?'

'It's a bit like a corny love song, isn't it? I loved you before I knew you. Before I knew your face, your sex, before I knew your character or anything. All that mattered was that we were related. Isn't love more specific than that?'

'Be careful what you say. Your child absorbs *everything*.' She kisses her hand and rubs it into her giant belly. 'I tell Felix that I love him all the time, *don't I, gorgeous*!'

Felix has had a name for several months, ever since he revealed his gender, but you remain a vaguer entity. In company, I refer to you as the Beast, or Bruce, or Bazza, gargoyle names to deflect the evil eye. Now, as Grace coos at her belly, I try to imagine you asleep in the adjacent room. A baby, instead of a filing cabinet. And not just any baby: *my* baby.

No, I do not see it.

Grace turns back to me. 'Have you thought about what sort of child you want to have?'

'Do we get to choose?'

'You choose the upbringing.'

'So what do you want?'

'Extroverted and athletic, but at the same time a poet.' She smiles fondly, as though describing a new lover. 'Bilingual, definitely. A surfer.'

I have not dared script your birth yet, let alone design you. Perhaps I just want you to be happy, as mothers claim. But can that be right? Would I be happy with a happy paedophile?

'Surely you have some expectations?' she persists.

'It seems likely that our child will be short-sighted.'

Somewhere, I am developing other suspicions about you, but I will not articulate them. It is part superstition, but part something else, too. I want to protect you from my ambition. I never want you to feel its edge. So perhaps I do love you, already, even more than I love myself. I just find it hard to say.

Most nights I dream of you. Frantic dreams stirred up by the industry in my belly. One night, the doctor pulls you out early, shaves you of lanugo, and you race around the room, barking like a poodle. Another night you are born a blank piece of paper, and when I swaddle you, I accidentally rip your corner.

The best and most vivid dream is that you are born, and you are a boy. A boy! Your gender brings you into focus, gives you identity. You are a real baby. Can it be true?

We can find out your gender at our next ultrasound, if we choose.

'Don't do it!' Fiona insists. Her brow furrows threateningly, as during political argument. 'I really feel strongly about this. Some mystery has to be preserved. And believe me – labour is so challenging that you *need* that extra surprise at the end.'

I defer to her expertise, but hope I might accidentally catch a glimpse of your sex anyway.

'Are you sure?' asks Sash, when I invite her to the ultrasound.

'Of course. Safety in numbers. Just in case.'

'In case what?'

I do not say it, but in case you are a poodle or a blank piece of paper. Before I knew you were there, I had x-rays and CAT scans, drank too much wine, knocked back a cocktail of medications each night to go to sleep.

'Don't catastrophise,' she warns me. 'Women are baby-making machines.'

It is a clear winter morning when we drive to the clinic, and on the radio a Finnish violinist plays a glistening Vivaldi. For the first time, I allow myself to admit the scale of my ambition. To have a good pregnancy and a safe delivery. For you to be a healthy child. For you to have a happy and successful and long life. For there to be no apocalypse in your lifetime, or in the lifetime of your children, or grandchildren. Is there no end to my greed?

'Don't catastrophise,' Sash repeats from the back seat.

At the clinic, bulging women are wedged into the sofas, some with partners, some alone. The glass doors open and release a dazed, love-struck couple; another woman is called in.

Baba calls. 'News, please.'

'No news yet.'

'Drat.' She hangs up.

I pick up a gossip magazine, in which celebrity mums reveal flawless post-baby bodies. They have never felt so beautiful, or so fulfilled. Motherhood has given them the confidence to do their best work. 'The more chaos the better!' carols an actress with blow-waved hair and porcelain skin. I read the article several times, willing it to be true.

Sash leans over my shoulder. 'Mother hobbyists.'

Each time the glass doors open, my heartbeat accelerates. Then another woman is called in, and it slows a little, never quite returning to where it was before. The waiting room thins out until my impatience to meet you becomes a physical need. My bladder is optimally full, as instructed, but after an hour I go to the toilet, and when I return the nurse calls us in.

I climb on to the bed and lie on my back, naked beneath the pale blue gown. As the doctor pulls on a pair of gloves, I can feel my naivety pressing down on me, palpable as the lump on my belly. She rubs on some gel and then applies the transducer, squinting at the monitor.

'Did you empty your bladder?'

'Sorry. It was a long wait.'

She sighs, moving the transducer elsewhere. The images on the screen are fleeting, nebulous, bearing no resemblance to human form.

'Is everything okay?' asks Nicholas.

'I'm not getting a clear picture.'

I rehearse the possibilities. That you were only a phantom. That you have somehow gone missing in the womb. 'Is there definitely something in there?'

'Of course.'

In my imagination I can see you clearly, swivelling your mouth towards her impatient fingers, but none of this registers on the monitor.

'Get up and move around. Try to get that baby to turn around.'

I climb off the bed, ashamed of my poor uterine discipline. How do I get you to turn around? Nicholas and Sash shrug back at me, so I improvise three half-hearted star jumps and a downward dog, and then climb back on to the bed.

After a couple of perfunctory movements, the doctor puts the transducer away. 'I don't have time for this. Come back later, when you've got that baby in a better position.'

'Sorry,' I tell Sash, as we wait at the pedestrian crossing. Cars speed past us, glinting in the early afternoon sun.

'Don't be *stoopid*.'

My mind loops around, searching for a deal I could make to secure a good scan. A deal with whom? With the devil?

'Don't catastrophise,' she reminds me. 'You're descended from an unbroken line of successful breeders.'

'It's just that when things start going wrong, they usually continue to go wrong.'

'Not true at all,' says Nicholas, steering me across the road. But for the first time I have a clear view of life as a parent. Today is only the rehearsal for a lifetime of worry. I remember what Fiona told me, when she brought Matilda home: *I will never be happy again.*

The phone rings.

'News, please,' demands Baba.

'The baby won't turn around.'

'Stubborn, just like its father. Call me when you have something.'

At the 7-Eleven, I get stuck trying to choose between Burger Rings and Cheezels – *there must be a right choice; there is always a right choice.*

'For God's sake,' says Sash, seizing the Burger Rings. Back in the waiting room, I suck the worry out of each small ring until it dissolves to cardboard in my mouth.

When the doctor calls us back, there is a sheen of perspiration on her face. 'Let's hope we can all do a bit better this time.'

I lie down hopelessly, knowing you will not have turned, as she stares at the monitor with pursed lips.

'That's it! We're doing an internal.' She snaps on a pair of clear plastic gloves. 'Touch your feet against each other, and let your knees fall to the side.'

She produces a long wand, lubricates it and plunges it between my legs. I flinch, grabbing Nicholas's hand, as she steers it like a joystick, staring grimly at the monitor. Would you go into this business if you hated vaginas, and the work of vaginas? Every time she moves the wand, I feel newly pinched inside, and I realise something basic. This pregnancy, which I had been construing as a spiritual, metaphysical experience, is in fact a bestial process. It will turn me back into a body. Over the next months, there will be any number of gentle and impatient strangers trafficking with my vagina. I squeeze Nicholas's hand more tightly, juicing it of its comfort, and realise something else. In six months I will be going through labour. This discomfort is only the mildest foretaste of what lies ahead. How much use will this warm, beloved hand be to me then? Like death, labour is something I have to go through alone. Or with one other person only, in our flimsy craft of two. There is no safety in numbers, after all. There is only me, and then there is you.

A final pinch, and a picture flickers up on the screen. It is you! You, who have been evading capture. You are fluid, composed of smoke or air, morphing between ectoplasm and skeleton. It is a cosmic strip show: a flash of spine, and then a ribcage, clean as a fish. Who is laying these bones down, one by one? Is it me who is making you, or are you making yourself? You spin around and reveal your profile and I gasp, because you are even more beautiful than I had dared imagine. Your serene brow, the dip of your nose, your small self-possessed mouth. She captures you by the scruff of your neck to take your measurements, and then zooms in to your hardening skull, to the two halves of your brain, nestled in their twin cavities. It is both awesome and terrifying: why must there be so many component parts, so many places where things could go wrong? Next we dive down your torso in cross-section, past your two dormant lungs and the black cavity of your stomach to the great motor of your heart. It is so private in here; surely we should not be looking. She picks out the passage of blood in red, so that we can see its great work, its relentless gush between you and me, that pulse by which we first knew you. Then she pans out again to the outside of your body, to your busy, slender arms and that tiny star of your hand, waving at us – yes, I am sure you are waving at us – and you dance away, back to non-existence.

She removes the transducer and returns my body to me. 'Looks fine to me.' It is the greatest understatement of my life. 'We'll process these measurements for chromosomal abnormality.'

At home, I watch your DVD repeatedly, until I have you memorised. Two days later, I call my obstetrician for the results.

'Let's see,' says her receptionist. 'Bear with me while I find the right file.'

I have looked inside your body and seen the beginnings of existence, but right now I am as vulnerable to your future as any medieval peasant.

'Oh yes – here it is. The risk of chromosomal abnormality is 1 in 6754.'

I write this wondrous statistic down on a piece of paper, fold it up and carry it in my wallet. It is first prize in the only lottery. These are big numbers – big enough, surely, to protect you from more than chromosomal abnormality. Big enough to keep you safe through childhood, and adolescence, and beyond, to spare you heartbreak, grief, mental illness. Big enough to guarantee you a long, happy and successful life, whatever success comes to mean for you. Big enough to keep the apocalypse at bay, in your lifetime, in your grandchildren's lifetime, and even in the lifetime of your grandchildren's grandchildren.

PORRIDGE

By eighteen weeks, your hearing is switched on. How does it feel, suddenly to have a functioning sound system? Is there a moment when sound is no longer only a vibration against your skin, but a direct fright to the brain? It must be loud in there, lodged between bladder and bowel. Human bodies are noisy places: the regular gong of heartbeat; the seismic rumbles of intestines; the great waterfalls of piss. One day, my flesh will appal you, as that of a stranger after a mistaken intimacy. *Close the toilet door, Mum.* But not yet. Right now, we are almost one.

As your senses become keener, I feel crowded by the sensory world. My piano was tuned a week ago, but already it has turned rotten. Is this you, demanding a perfected world into which to be born? Pop visits on the way home from a book tour of Germany, rubbing his forefinger against the rough skin of his thumb as he speaks.

'Can you please stop that?'

'What?'

'That unbearable *thumb friction*.'

He laughs, but then the fleshy sandpaper starts up again and I have to flee the room.

Visiting my obstetrician becomes the highlight of each fortnight. As Monica places her stethoscope on my belly, I feel the excitement of a long-distance call to a beloved relative, although you always say the same thing: *ka-boom, ka-boom*.

'Have you given thought to a birth plan?' Monica asks, as she puts the stethoscope away.

'Only that I want an epidural.'

She nods. 'There are risks, especially with your bleeding disorder.'

'What sort of risks?'

'Paralysis. We'll need to run tests.'

'My friend told me that pain was a social construct.' This comes out sounding more hopeful than I had intended. 'She says it can be overcome using hypnosis.'

Calmly she appraises my face. 'To be frank, I've never seen a woman give birth without pain. When exactly did your friend give birth?'

'She hasn't yet.'

The tiniest hint of a smile washes over her eyes and forehead and then disappears. 'Why don't you ask your friend about it again, after she has given birth?'

At nineteen weeks, something comes into focus inside me, and I feel you move. A flutter that is clearly not digestive. The faintest tickle of wings.

'There's a kick,' I say and place Nicholas's hand on my belly, always a second too late.

Sash takes me to a bar with her glamorous friends, and we push through the crowd to a table by the window.

'Have you decided on a name?' asks Emma, a fashion designer.

'Not really.'

'Would you like some suggestions?' I struggle to hear her over the music. 'Don't you think Yoyo is gorgeous? Or what about Lupus? Or even Ankle?'

The conversation shifts to parties, to foxy men, to trips to New York. Why would anyone want to talk about such things when they could talk about babies? I sip on my mineral water with its small portion of lime, realising that it was alcohol all this time that made life interesting.

'I thought of another name,' says Emma. 'Bastard.'

'Bastard?'

She laughs. '*Custard.*'

I have never been an accomplished lip-reader. 'That's an unusual name.'

'Didn't you kiss a Custard one time?' my sister asks her. 'Wasn't he married?'

They are away again, and I feel both nauseous and incontinent. Getting to the bathroom will be impossible, so I will just have to stop drinking mineral water. But there is nothing else to do. The waiter brings a plate of zucchini flowers to the table. He is tall and aloof, with a tattoo zigzagging down his muscled arm. The fact that he is good-looking does not improve my night in any way.

'What exactly are you looking for in a name?' Emma asks.

'A name as transparent as water. A name that imposes no expectations on the face beneath.'

'There is no such name,' Sash tells me.

The zucchini flowers emit a radioactive cloud of spice and oil, and I feel a passionate yearning to be home. To be sitting on the sofa in my flannelette pyjamas, eating milky porridge: pale, bland baby food that resembles the new texture of my flesh. To be porridge, eating porridge. The music presses in like panic. *Get out*, it thuds, *get out, go home, get out, go home.*

'You've changed,' Sash says as she finds me a taxi. 'You've gone from being the most tolerant person I know to the most intolerant. You've leap-frogged everybody I know, even Baba. It's spectacular.'

I know she is right, that this pregnancy is changing more than just my body. Who am I, if not my preferences and characteristics? Am I still myself, or have I metamorphosed permanently into something else, some tandem being of me-you?

The days accumulate like fatigue. Every afternoon, I steal away to the university swimming pool. *Careful baby don't fall out!* the housekeeper warns me if I pass her on the staircase of the college where we live. But the water neutralises my pregnancy. It returns my old body to me, releasing the weight on my stomach, the weight on my thinking, the weight hovering over my future. As I trace lap after lap, there seems no good reason to stop swimming ever, but then a small chorus starts up in my ears – mothers and aunts and grandmothers. *Don't overdo it.* I realise I am slipping into old, bad habits, so I heave myself out of the pool and rest on the tiles. The attendant delicately turns his head away, as I catch my breath, beached once more in pregnancy.

VIDEO

At twenty-two weeks, you have a mouth full of tiny tooth buds, and the faintest traces of fingerprints waiting under your skin. Each week I receive a pregnancy e-newsletter, telling me how I am feeling: *At twenty-two weeks pregnant, you may be feeling slightly less dainty and more bulky.*

Schoolboys now stand for me on the tram, and I gladly sit down. As I lumber through the university, I glimpse a writer I know, jogging with his dog, and feel a fleeting envy. *Of course, he's a man, he is only one.*

'You're pregnant!' my piano tuner announces. 'I can tell from your complexion.'

'Thank you.' I am pleased to be blooming.

He squints in closer. 'Your skin is very dull. And there's a glazed-over sheen to your eyes.'

At pre-natal classes later that week, I see that he is right: the pregnant glow is a chivalrous fiction. My fellow pregnant waddle into the elevator beside me to parallel park. Nobody makes eye contact, as if reluctant to be drawn into a complicity, a sisterhood of the knocked-up. As the lift moves up to the second floor, I study these other women in the mirror. There is something shameless about their large, tumorous stomachs: declarations of animality, of sexual appetite. Can this really be what I look like, too?

'Today's first session will be on pain relief,' the midwife announces when we arrive. With her sandals and shiny face, she seems too young to induct us into motherhood.

'We'll start by getting to know each other. What are you most looking forward to about having a child?'

'Kicking a ball around the park,' volunteers a man at the back.

'Baby couture!' says the woman next to him. She drapes a beringed hand over her neat spherical bump, elegant as a Fabergé egg. 'There's some *gorgeous* stuff out there.'

Teaching you words, I think. There is something so private about this, so sacred, I am not sure if I can say it in front of strangers. *Naming the world for you.*

'I'm really just looking forward to having children,' offers the woman beside me, hesitantly. 'We were trying for nine years, and we lost some babies, and we thought it wasn't going to happen. This was our first round of IVF.' She clutches her husband's hand. 'And we're having twins.'

This is the first time it happens. Even before I know I am moved, the tears are streaming down my face. They are tidal, irresistible, so that when it comes to my turn, I cannot speak.

After morning tea, the midwife projects a diagram of pain-relief options on the whiteboard.

'It's up to you and your doctor to decide on a strategy. All I can do is offer the following information. If you choose nitrous oxide, there's some evidence that it might lead to future amphetamine abuse in your child. On the other hand, pethidine might cause future opiate dependency.'

Amphetamines/opiates? I write on my notepad, hesitating over it with my pen as if choosing the nursery wallpaper.

'An epidural is unlikely to have an adverse effect on the child, but in certain cases it can cause paralysis in the mother.'

I cross out *amphetamines/opiates* and begin a new birth plan. The blood tests, surely, will be fine. I will have an epidural.

'A word of warning. Many doctors perform unnecessary caesareans. I'm telling you, it's a national disgrace. There's no reason why you can't give birth naturally. Women have been doing it for centuries. Let's watch a video, so you can see what I'm talking about.'

So this is the labour video. There will be no escape. After the opening credits and ambient birthing music, the camera focuses on a young woman. She has frizzy orange hair and a plain, sensible face, and speaks with a Canadian accent.

'For me there was never an option. It was always going to be a natural birth, in front of my family.'

She sips a cup of herbal tea, rocking languidly on an exercise ball. I am not sure why I resent her.

'Now we're coming up to the first labour pains,' the midwife announces. Something passes over the woman's face. She scrunches up her forehead and then lets it go, and glances over to the camera, as if catching her reflection in a mirror. When the next contraction arrives, she breathes more gutturally. An attendant brings her a glass of water, but she pushes it away.

'This video is not in real time,' the midwife interrupts. 'But you can tell that she is moving through the first stage of labour.'

There is a flurry of activity on the screen. The attendant removes her underpants and holds them up to the camera, revealing a small bloodied slug.

'That's the mucous plug, or *bloody show*,' says the midwife.

The attendant takes the mucous plug to an adjacent room, to loud cheers. Someone mentions a Tupperware container. I had not known of the mucous plug, nor that you were supposed to keep it as a pet. It is a lot of information to take in at once.

As the video progresses, the woman no longer checks in with the camera. Her waters break, fanning out on the bed before her. As the contractions become more frequent, her experience becomes more interior; her face produces expressions I cannot read, that I have no register for. She stands abruptly and paces the room, and then presses herself against a wall, groaning. I glance at the women in the room around me, silent as animals in an abattoir.

'We are now in Transition,' announces the midwife, pausing the video. 'During Transition, many women feel like dying.'

I had not heard of Transition either, this particular purgatory reserved for women. Another measure of my naivety.

The woman's features become blurred, twisting away from the human. I no longer resent her in any way. Instead, I resent this breezy midwife, who will not be Transitioning anytime soon; resent any biological system that extracts such a price from women; resent any human being who expects to be born, regardless.

'Others say they want to go home or go to sleep forever,' continues the midwife. 'Or even that they no longer want to have a baby.'

The woman stumbles back to her bed as her family files in for the birth: bushy-bearded men in trucker hats, uncles and cousins and brothers. One of them carries a can of Pepsi and glances around for somewhere to put it.

'We now come to the pushing stage,' says the midwife, and the woman is no longer sobbing but bellowing. The tendons of her neck push out like wire, and her eyes roll backwards into her head. I wonder if I have ever seen such effort.

'Sometimes it is accompanied by a burning sensation.'

The woman bawls and she whimpers and she roars, and before her yawning vagina the men are utterly still. After minutes of this noise and this pain, a wrinkled crown appears, which morphs into a head, and then slides out as a human.

We all gasp, as if taken by surprise. The family whoops and delivers high fives, and our class breaks into applause. Again I am crying, out of love for this red angry child, and for her Canadian mother, and for every expectant parent in this room and their hope for the human project.

Afterwards, the placenta arrives without fanfare. It is taken into the kitchen, presumably in search of Tupperware. The newborn baby crawls up to his mother's nipple and the video comes to an end. When the midwife turns on the lights and asks for questions, everyone is silent.

'In that case, that will be all for today,' she says, her voice gentler now. 'Some of you will be back in the next few weeks for our class on breastfeeding. And if I don't see you again: *good luck*.'

In the toilets on the way out, the women steer around each other like ocean liners. At the hand dryer, I bump stomachs with another woman, and we bounce apart. There is a surprising intimacy to the transaction: the tightness, the tumescence of her girth. We apologise to each other politely, and move out into the night.

LATCH

At twenty-three weeks, your face is finished, the face by which we will know you. Your ears have swung into position, and you are growing eyelashes and a transparent crop of hair. If you were born now, you might be viable, but I would like you to stay inside a while longer.

We receive an ecstatic phone call from Bruno and go to visit Grace in hospital. She is propped up on pillows, authoritative as a queen, breastfeeding her new baby.

'How was labour?'

'Fine.'

'Did the hypnosis work?'

She smiles her magnificent smile. 'I tried to tolerate it for as long as I could, but it was impossible. I felt imprisoned by pain, trapped like an animal. As soon as I had the epidural, everything changed. It was a blessing. Promise me you'll have one.'

'I'll try.'

She detaches Felix from her breast and folds him into a burp.

'Would you like to hold him?'

I reach out and take her baby. He is both baggy and compact, with the perfect features of an elf. In about seventeen weeks I will be holding you like this. What will it mean to have you in my hands? Will I merely have to feed and change and dress and wash you, and keep you safe? Is that all?

Felix scrunches his fruit-bat face and mewls, and Grace reaches for him, reflexively. I realise there is more. In four months, we will be your most important people. There will be no-one else to hand you to, as I hand Felix back to his mother now, and then say goodbye.

At twenty-four weeks, I wake to find a fine outline of brown around each of my nipples, bulls-eyes for your mouth, applied by Nature's deft crayon as I slept. We return to the hospital for our second pre-natal class, on breastfeeding. A heavy-set woman storms into the room, and zips open a sports bag, revealing a stash of small human limbs.

'My name is Lavinia and I'm a Lactation Consultant.'

'Wouldn't you love to be able to drop that into conversation?' titters the woman behind me.

'I'm glad to see some husbands here,' Lavinia continues. 'You would be amazed at the indifference of some men. As if breasts were *playthings*, rather than nature's most perfect source of nutrition.'

She fixes me with a ferocious glare, and I wonder if I have always been too frivolous about my breasts. 'Women, your *breasts* are amazing.' The word is pronounced onomatopoeically, with rolled R and savoured vowels, as though tracing a large breast in the air. Then she reaches into her bag, pulls out a breast-shaped stress ball and squeezes it voluptuously. 'Mother Nature knows what she is doing, which is why we call her *Mother*. When your baby is born, she should be placed immediately on your stomach. She will crawl up to your breasts – that's right, *crawl up herself* – and fix herself to the nipple. It's called turning the tap on. Nobody needs to weigh a child as soon as she is born. That's just about men wanting to convert rich human life into numbers.'

She passes the breast ball around the room. No-one seems quite sure what to do with it. I give it a few desultory squeezes and hand it to the man on my right.

'Let's start by talking about when your milk comes in. It's crucial that you have appropriate supportive apparatus.'

This time, she removes a baggy white garment from her bag. With surprising, shimmying grace, she pulls it over her head, threads an arm into each hole and wriggles it over her formidable bosom.

'My own invention,' she explains.

It is a peculiar item of clothing, comprising two white pouches, each cradling a large load of breast. It is not quite a bra, and yet somehow familiar.

'Not a *glamorous* item, perhaps, but extremely practical. Constructed, quite simply, from two pairs of *plus-size underpants*.'

There seems to be a loud whoosh from the room: the collective evaporation of libido. Gone – perhaps forever? It is not enough to wear gigantic underpants that look like nappies: you must now wear them on your *breasts*. She shrugs off the underpants-bra and passes it around the room for closer study. The man in front of us makes a detailed sketch, with schematic safety pins at key structural points. Beside me, Nicholas looks stoical.

'We now come to *procedure*. I will ask for your full attention, because if you don't commit it to memory now, you won't have a hope when you've just given birth.'

She reaches again into her sports bag and this time pulls out an infant-sized doll.

'Begin by holding your child in readiness, shoulders supported with right forearm. Always remember: chest to chest, nose to nipple. Gather the areola with thumb and forefinger, lead baby with chin, bottom lip and tongue first *always,* and then flick the nipple in, forming an acute angle with upper palate.'

I feel the panic of a boy scout failing to understand a complex knot.

'Feed the nipple further into the mouth and bingo! You have established latch. *Latch is critical.*'

She places her child down on the floor, and carries the sports bag around the room, dealing out children. I receive a tousle-haired baby girl with alarmed blue eyes. She is stiff and unyielding and nothing as I imagine you to be. There is nowhere on my body where she might belong. Am I supposed to attach my nipple to her mouth? Or should it be more like an air kiss: approximate and gestural? Wordlessly, Lavinia repositions my arms, pressing the child's cold plastic mouth into my chest.

'I'll ask you to continue to nurse through the following video. Though I should warn you, I get a little impatient because of a baby called Sam. It's not Sam's fault, mind you, he gives his mother plenty of opportunities, but at the key moment she *fails to latch*.'

As I hold my plastic child to my breast, I watch a woman with a live baby on the screen. The baby struggles and flails, swatting at her breast with small frantic hands. Beside her, a Lactation Consultant makes consoling noises, bunching up her nipple, aiming it unsuccessfully into the child's hungry mouth.

'Chest to chest! Nose to nipple!' barks Lavinia. 'Here comes her chance. And that's what I mean! Sam's mouth is open, and she missed, completely. Come on, girl! *Flick that nipple in!*'

The woman on the screen starts to weep, and I feel dismayed to be a human being, sitting in this room nursing a plastic doll, trying to remember what it is to be an animal.

MOZART

At twenty-eight weeks we enter the third trimester, but your life has clearly already begun. In bed, I park my belly against Nicholas's back, and you wake us both with the force of your karate kick. *Pow.* When the alarm sounds in the morning, you jerk awake, frightened as a fish. What do you dream of in there? Different shades of peach and black?

The students hold a party downstairs at college, and all night the carpet thumps with a relentless beat. I sleep in snatches and wake in fright, feeling your agitation in our shared blood. *The drums are coming.* Who am I? Where am I? Can I really have another human growing inside me?

Morning arrives, and with it the consolation of the piano. *You must play Mozart for baby every day*, my teacher prescribes. *And Bach, of course, and some Chopin. Music that brings you to life.* When not at the piano I sing Mozart in my head. Can you hear it there too? *Such a lucky baby*, people tell me after concerts, *listening to music all the time.* Semiquavers start making me breathless; during my final recital, I have to pause between movements to recover. But it is less lonely out there on the stage. The audience has become closer, has moved inside me. I feel I am listening differently, with your ears as well as my own.

By twenty-nine weeks, you are practising your breath, inhaling and exhaling small quantities of fluid. Sometimes it goes down the wrong way and I feel the abrupt rhythm of your hiccups.

We are invited to opening night of the opera, and I make a final attempt at glamour. Tricked out in chiffon, I am as large and gaudy as a circus tent. On the escalator, my belly bumps against the other patrons like a *faux pas*; Nicholas helps me disembark, and they swiftly swim away, in their bespoke suits and gleaming velvets.

It is a relief to claim our seats, close to the orchestra pit. And now the house-lights dim, and the overture begins. Back to first principles. Here I am a woman, a pregnant woman, watching an opera. I thought pregnancy might make more sense when it happened to me, but it remains as implausible as ever. There are several places where my imagination fails me. The shape of my future life. The shape of your life inside me. The fact that you are real.

What will it be like, our new life? Will I be forced into domesticity, into a practical version of womanhood I have always fled? Perhaps this will feel like a homecoming, after so many long days out in the world. But my larger anxiety is this: will there still be room, in our new life, for this room in my head?

The music takes flight, and my flesh slips away. In front of us, the coiffed heads glow silver and gold, like treasure. Some of them nod to the music, others maintain a rapt stillness. What will you make of this, little bean? Each of the faces in the audience – weary, preoccupied, intent – concealing its own universe of thoughts. Some leaning into the music like sustenance; others accepting it as their due, like the laundered furs and silks they left in the cloakroom. Some performing corporate takeovers behind veiled eyes; others vexed by the tempo, which was brisker last year at Covent Garden. And each of them – bewilderingly – once a pregnancy. Each of them physical evidence of a sexual act: thrilling, dutiful, painful or tender. How certain they seem, these wealthy burghers of Melbourne, for creatures so random.

I turn back to Nicholas and study his profile in the half-light. This dear man, this man who, unbelievably, was once a stranger. Merged now, for the duration. His mouth sets as he feels me watching him, and then he nods back towards the front, towards the pale flash of the conductor's hands. But I am not ignoring Mozart. The music encompasses all of this: the abundance, the absurdity, the wonder.

Perhaps I should pity you, shortly to be born, to be parcelled into identity, but I do not. Because this music is saying something else.

Can you hear it? Are you still listening?

Welcome, it calls out to you. *Welcome to life.*

HYDRANGEAS

By thirty-two weeks you are moving less, as your Olympic-sized swimming pool shrinks to snug cocoon. The outside world, this parallel dimension that will soon suck you up, is coming closer.

I throw myself into a flurry of housework, as though expecting a visiting dignitary. It is critical that the silverware be cleaned before your arrival, that all paperwork be properly filed and archived. Baba flies over from Adelaide to help prepare and takes me to the Breastfeeding Association for the purchase of maternity bras.

'An interesting case,' the shop assistant says dubiously, measuring my chest. 'Very hard to categorise.' She fetches a handful of maternity bras, which resemble no underwear I have known. They might be abseiling equipment, with trapdoors and pouches, secret entry points, straps for extra reinforcement. I apply them gingerly to my uncategorisable bosom.

'You know the rules,' Baba calls into the change-room. 'No eliminating unless I've seen it first.'

As I parade for Baba, I view my new body in the mirror. Somewhere within it lies my old body, as scaffolding for these giant, rude appendages: this bulge that contains you, these bulbous breasts.

'That looks like a *good sensible* brassiere,' she declares. 'What do you think?'

I have no opinion about sensible brassieres or anything else. My brain has been absorbed into a fat suit, possibly never to re-emerge.

'We'll take the black and the beige,' she tells the sales assistant. 'And that white singlet with the detachable straps.'

As the woman rings up my purchase, I eye the chair by the counter, making secret calculations. Sitting down would be a relief, yes, but such a commitment should not be entered into lightly due to the high cost of standing back up. The woman is brisk and efficient, and I am pleased with my decision to remain upright.

At home, Nicholas takes me aside. 'Before you buy anything else, I need to show you something.' He opens a cupboard in his study, and a stash of tiny clothes tumbles out. Every payday for the last six months he has ordered you something beautiful: tear-shaped bibs, screen-printed t-shirts, soft kimonos of organic cotton. Baba launders them as I sleep, and then irons them in the next room. When I wake up she is singing, in a way I have not heard her sing for years.

The results of my blood tests arrive, and Monica reads me the letter from the haematologist: '*There is an increased risk of epidural haemotoma, and epidural anaesthesia should be avoided.'*

'There are other options,' she reassures me, as my only birth plan evaporates. 'Pethidine. A caesarean under a general anaesthetic.'

I remembered the sandalled midwife from pre-natal classes – her shining, virtuous face – warning against future opiate addiction, against unnecessary caesareans. Why can't the experts agree? Surely there should be a master plan by now. It is not as if childbirth were just invented.

'I remember you expressed some interest in hypnosis. It might be worth exploring that further.'

So I may yet be the proud owner of a natural, drug-free birth. There is possibly a delicious irony to this somewhere. Back home, I call Grace's hypnosis workshop and make an appointment. They send me a brochure:

The word pain has no place in the birth experience. Through hypnosis, you will discover that birth sensations can be pleasurable, and should never be confused with pain.

I concentrate on this statement, reading it aloud to myself, trying to absorb it into my belief system. Is it possible that women have been crying wolf all these years?

'Can you keep your sense of humour through labour?' I ask Fiona.

She considers this. 'Imagine working out at the gym until your muscles are in meltdown. And then being possessed by a demon who forces you to perform another twenty thousand repetitions. If you feel like cracking a joke, then sure, hats off to you, funny girl.'

I cancel my hypnosis appointment. If I am not a true believer, there seems to be no point.

At thirty-four weeks, it is clear that this pregnancy must soon stop. It can go no further. Your bottom is a tight fist under my diaphragm; your feet leave imprints around my sides.

'You need to make yourself bigger than the pain,' a woman tells me at a book launch. 'It helps to vocalise, and it helps even more if your partner vocalises with you.'

Back home, I discuss this with Nicholas. Should we rehearse our vocalisations before the event?

'I imagine it's more an improvisational thing,' he suggests.

Sash calls. 'Do you have a birth plan yet?'

'Only a vague plan, centred around improvisational yodelling.'

'You're going to need more than that. I've found a list of psychologists around Melbourne who perform hypnosis.'

'Are you suggesting I have a *birth experience*?'

Her voice takes on a professional solicitude. 'I think you should arm yourself with any tools available. And a psychologist could offer some useful techniques, without maintaining labour is painless.'

'Does hypnosis work even if you don't believe in it?'

'You should believe in it.'

'Do you?'

She swallows audibly. 'Up to a point. Studies show that hypnosis can be very helpful. Not for everyone, but for certain people.'

'What sort of people?'

She considers this for a moment. 'Suggestible people.'

I try a number of the psychologists on her list, none of whom can see me for several weeks, until I get through to Vera in the Dandenongs, an hour's drive away.

'Do you offer hypnosis to prepare for birth?'

'Do I offer *what* to prepare for *what*?'

'Hypnosis. To help with childbirth.'

'Oh yes. I offer hypnosis all the time to help with childbirth.'

'Could I make an appointment?'

'Come anytime. Tomorrow, first thing?'

The following morning it is raining heavily, so Nicholas offers to drive. As we are leaving, there is a giant peal of thunder and the dog starts howling, so we bring him too. The rain becomes torrential as we approach the mountains, until we seem to be driving directly into a cloud. *You are now at your destination*, intones the GPS. It is not the professional hypnosis clinic I was expecting but instead resembles a gingerbread cottage, with neat eaves and lolly-pink shutters. I leave Nicholas and the dog in the car and run to the front door.

A large woman throws open the door before I have removed my finger from the doorbell. Her pencilled-on eyebrows lend her a look of astonishment.

'Anna, I must assume. I am Vera.'

She wears a beige twinset with red patent-leather Mary Janes that are clearly several sizes too small.

'Come along, then!'

She hobbles through the kitchen past a table, where a large textbook lies open at *Hypnosis*. I follow her into a small living room, decorated with macramé wall-hangings.

'Please, lie down on my hypnosis couch.' She hastily removes a television remote control, sits on the armchair opposite and stares at me significantly.

'Before we begin, I must ask: why are you so fearful of giving birth?'

'It's not that I'm fearful, particularly. It's just that I understand it's a painful experience.'

'I find that *very revealing*.'

She holds my gaze until I wonder if she is hypnotising me, and then nods abruptly.

'We'll start with a straightforward hypnosis exercise. Did you bring a tape?'

'No.'

'I have a spare, but of course I will have to charge extra for it.' She takes a cassette tape out of her cupboard, dusts it off and puts it in the tape deck. When she presses *play*, Bollywood music fills the room.

'Oh no, you *certainly* cannot have that one.'

She takes another tape and slides it in. This time, a man's voice declaims something in Polish. She grunts and presses *record*.

'Lie back and close your eyes, and concentrate on your breathing. *In and out, in and out.*'

There it is, the breath: reliable after all. Though subject to a certain self-consciousness when observed. How much does one inhale, usually? And how long a pause before the release?

'Don't seek to control it. Just listen. I am now going to count backwards from ten. With every number, I would like you to become more fully relaxed. *Ten ... Nine ... Eight ...*'

There is a distant clap of thunder. I hope Nicholas and the dog are safe, out there in the storm.

'*Seven ... Six ...*'

As she counts down, the outlines of this room blur, and the storm recedes, along with my concern for Nicholas and the dog, until once again it is only you and me.

'Imagine a garden. Any garden. A garden from your childhood.'

It is your Great-Grandma Moggy's garden, the garden Baba grew up in.

'What can you see?'

I can see all the grass of that garden, and I can see all the sky that garden contains. I wonder if I am being hypnotised, if my sister is right and I am a suggestible person.

'What else can you see?'

The watercolours of Moggy's hydrangeas crowding the fence, in mauve and sky-blue and a rare lime-green, like a hybrid of petal and palest leaf. The dark pond, lit for a moment by the goldfish when I disturb the water with a stick.

'What can you hear?'

A cockatoo crash-landing in the golden elm, making no attempt to brake. The murmur of the grown-ups. An outburst from my uncle, and everyone laughs. There is probably a sponge cake, the red of the raspberries leaching into the cream by now.

'You may find that thoughts or anxieties drift into your mind.'

Certain things lurk around the edge of this garden. The fernhouse, brown and moist, inhabited by animal ferns with long hairy tails. Other things, too. The knowledge that one day this house will be sold and the garden subdivided, against Moggy's wishes. That one day these adults will stop laughing together.

'Just let them go and return to the garden.'

Above me, the giant elm tree separates the Adelaide sky into shades of gold and lemon on my face. It is the only sky I know.

'Stay there now. Rest in that garden.'

I would like to show you this garden, but you will have your own gardens and I wonder what they might look like. Various possibilities merge until I am breastfeeding a puppy with floppy ears in a pond and a swan wraps its long neck around me. Nicholas swims ahead in the orange robes of a Hare Krishna and then I remember I am supposed to be in Moggy's garden and I return to the golden elm. Somewhere a woman is counting backwards from ten. Over there is the sunny front lawn for somersaults, and the wide verandah for the staging of plays. *There must be a beginning, and a middle, and an end,* says Baba. *Especially an end.*

When the woman gets to one, I open my eyes and find myself in a small living room. Opposite, a mantelpiece sags under a load of miniature Chinamen.

'You were successfully hypnotised.'

'I thought perhaps I dozed off.'

'No. You certainly did not.' She passes me a glass of water, and watches with interest as I sip.

'I notice you are not wearing a wedding ring. Is your fear of giving birth equated with your fear of marriage?'

Somewhere, alarm bells go off. But I still have one foot in Moggy's garden, the taste of sleep in my mouth. 'I don't think I'm fearful of marriage.'

'Did your parents have a happy marriage?'

'They divorced ten years ago.' I struggle to sit up. What is going on here, exactly? Does she know my parents? Did she hypnotise me in order to discover family secrets?

'How did you feel about that?'

'Sad. But they both seem happy now.'

'Is your partner supportive?'

'Very.' I think of Nicholas with relief. 'He drove me here.' It is only after I say this that I realise it is a mistake.

'We can make no further progress until I meet him.'

But Nicholas must not come into this room. His scepticism will undo me, will expel me from the garden.

'He can't leave the dog in this storm.'

She blinks, patiently. 'We need to ask what it is you are denying.'

'I'm not denying anything! I just want hypnosis to help me with the pain of childbirth.'

'We really need to examine your reluctance to involve your partner in this.'

It is my last chance to complete a birth plan, so I heave myself off the couch and lumber outside into the rain. Nicholas opens the car door, releasing a warm gust of dog breath.

'She wants to see you.'

'Why?'

'Suspend your disbelief. *Please*. I need this to work.'

We abandon the stricken dog and return inside. Vera is still sitting on her chair, but the textbook has migrated to the coffee table beside her. She nods at Nicholas and we perch, side by side, on the hypnosis couch.

'I find it very interesting and unusual that you are not married, and I would like you to explain for me why this is the case.'

It is like being summoned to the headmaster's office. The headmaster of marriage. Nicholas looks at me incredulously. I nudge him to answer.

'It's nothing against marriage. It just seems redundant when we're fully committed to each other.'

She leans forward in her chair and stares at him. 'How would you characterise your relationship with your father?'

I hold my breath. My pain-free labour depends on his compliance.

'I didn't know him well. My parents split up when I was very young.'

Outside there is a clap of thunder. I hear a single exploratory yelp.

'We're actually here for hypnosis training, rather than relationship guidance,' I point out.

'That's what we're getting to. You must understand, labour pains come in waves. The critical thing is ...' She picks up the book from her coffee table and reads. '*The critical thing is to feel as relaxed as possible between waves, to ensure you accumulate no anxiety about the wave to come. Move through the wave when it is there, but do not anticipate it.*'

It is a relief to be back on topic.

'This is where the exercise we just did comes in. One other thing I should mention.' She puts the book back down. 'Labour can be a deeply *sensuous* experience. You might find that you can enhance this through intimate massage throughout the labour experience.' She licks her lips. 'Some women like to have their breasts caressed as they are giving birth. Slowly, erotically ...'

There is another thunderclap. This time the dog starts howling like a wolf.

Nicholas stands up. 'I'm sorry, but we have to go.'

He runs back to the car, and Vera takes out her appointment diary, opening it to a blank page. 'We've made good progress, but we still have a lot to do.'

'I didn't bring my diary. Could I take the cassette?'

She ejects it from the tape deck but hesitates before giving it to me, as if she knows I do not plan to return.

'Thanks again.' I tug the cassette gently from her hand. 'The idea of not anticipating the anxiety is a really useful one. I'll practise the hypnosis at home.'

'You won't have a successful labour unless you get to the bottom of your marriage issues,' she calls after me, as I escape into the storm.

CONTRACTIONS

At thirty-seven weeks, you have officially dropped, and are engaged in position like an astronaut, ready for launch. When labour is not forthcoming, you pound violently against the escape hatch. Our friend Alice comes over for dinner and I tell her the story of my thwarted birth plan, building operatically to its climax: 'I have to give birth without an epidural!'

She looks at me bewildered, as though waiting for the punch line, and then becomes a little stern. 'Women all over the world give birth without an epidural,' she says carefully. 'They have done so through history and they continue to do so now.'

Grace didn't, I want to protest, *and neither did Fiona. It's not fair!* But I am embarrassed and change the subject. After she leaves, I take out my hypnosis tape and visit Moggy's garden. It seems to work, even though I remain unmarried.

The stairs are becoming unmanageable, so I spend most of my time on my hypnosis couch, or idly surfing the internet in search of a birth plan. Surely there are Cliff's Notes somewhere, or a Birth Plan for Dummies. One forum recommends a TENS machine, a portable transcutaneous electrical nerve stimulator. Electrodes attached to your back deliver small impulses, which might distract from the larger sensation of contractions. I disregard the mixed results of an Oxford University study and order one, express delivery. If my birth kit contains enough tools I only half believe in, it may yet work.

Your Uncle Daniel suffers from a pneumothorax – a collapsed lung – and has to cancel his Australian wedding. Instead he is married in London, and we watch the reception on Skype. Pop and Baba sit beside him on a sofa as he grins at Mutale, his serene and beautiful bride. As I watch and weep from afar, you kick downwards, with mounting impatience.

At my appointment with Monica, she performs an internal examination and grins. 'I wasn't expecting this. You've already dilated two centimetres. I can feel your baby's hair!'

You have hair! As I chuckle, you jiggle up and down in front of me in a true belly laugh. Back home, I pack a bag for the hospital, and there is a knock on the door. It is Nicholas, wielding a giant Christmas tree, breathless from carrying it up four flights of stairs. He presents it to me like a bouquet, and we wrestle it into a corner of the living room where it grazes the ceiling and fills the flat with its scent. After we decorate it, I sit beside it and listen to Mozart, feeling you dance inside me.

At book club, another friend turns up with her one-year-old baby. We have not seen her for over a year, ever since she was undone by motherhood. She seems to have transferred half of her body weight to her child, huge and placid as a panda.

'It's a bit like having a pet,' she says wearily. 'A high-maintenance pet.'

Back at home that night, I pick up my notebook, determined to complete this birth plan, but all I can come up with is a question: *Why is the dog so needy tonight?* He snuggles into the mountain of pillows I have arranged to support you, whimpering when I turn away, pressing his fretful nose into my back. You perform the usual kicks and wallops until I become aware of something else, a new sensation.

'I wonder if I'm in labour,' I announce to the bedroom.

Nicholas turns around. 'What's happening?'

'It feels like someone is chewing on my urethra.'

'That doesn't sound like labour. Go to sleep.'

I lie still, until the sensation becomes more distinct, coalescing into waves. Then I climb out of bed and turn on the computer, running a search on 'labour' to see what I might be feeling.

Contractions should occur at regular intervals and increase in frequency.

When the waves start radiating outward, I phone Baba, just back from London.

'Darling, that's probably just a Braxton Hicks.' Her voice is thick with sleep. 'Why don't you go back to bed and call me again in the morning?'

But I do not want to go back to bed. What if I accidentally sleep through your birth? Instead, I go into the living room and pick up Barack Obama's memoir. Every few pages I am interrupted by a wave. I wait for it to pass and then forget about it, as Vera instructed.

Nicholas comes out. 'If you seriously think you're in labour, we should ring the birth centre.'

'What's happening?' asks the nurse, over the phone.

'I'm having regular contractions.'

'Sweetie, I can tell by your voice that you're not in labour. Now there are women here who are giving birth and I have to go.'

I feel foolish, a labour wannabe, and Nicholas returns to bed. The waves now engage my stomach muscles, like crunches administered by remote control. Somewhere, a larrikin rooster begins his song, trumpeting a dawn that is still hours away. I attach the recently arrived TENS machine to my lower back and buzz it each time I have a contraction. The electrodes deliver a faint, sherbet-like tingle.

Now what? The only one who believes I am in labour is the dog, shadowing me around the flat. It seems an appropriate time to clean out my emails, so I move briskly through my inbox, archiving and replying and deleting. Look at me: the modern-day multi-tasking labourer! Perhaps the calm-birthers are right, and labour is not that bad, after all. Or maybe I have an unusually high threshold of pain, a talent of which I was previously unaware. The thought makes me exultant, and I quickly send emails to several of my friends. *Excuse me for a moment, while I just have a contraction … That's better. Back to what I was saying.* Gradually the sun warms the edges of the blind and the day begins in which you are going to be born.

Baba phones back. 'Do you still think you're in labour?'

'Yes.'

'I have to see a few patients this morning, but if you *really think you're in labour*, I'll try to get over in the early afternoon. How frequent are your contractions?'

'About every five minutes.'

'For God's sake, go to the birth clinic!'

I call the birth clinic back and speak to a different nurse. 'No, honey. You're too happy to be in labour.'

This would be the time to defrost some muffins for Nicholas, were I that sort of woman. Instead, I lie down on the hypnosis couch and listen to Vera's tape. Then I pick up Obama and continue reading. The contractions spread outwards, becoming a body-sized clamp that interrupts me every four pages, and then every three. I waddle back into the bedroom. 'I really think I'm in labour, but they won't let me come in.'

Nicholas jumps out of bed. 'This is ridiculous. I'm calling Monica and we're going in.'

In the car on the way to the hospital, I feel a trifle festive, as though on the way to a holiday. With any luck, there will be a bath in the birthing suite, and I can relax with a facial mask and read my book. Then, if all goes according to plan, the hospital will send us to a hotel for the recovery. I have been looking forward to this mini-break for some time, as a chance to catch up on some rest after the strain of pregnancy.

At the birth centre, three nurses are chatting at the reception. 'This one's mine,' says the tall blonde, and leads us into a small unadorned labour room, purpose-built like an interrogation chamber. She clicks an identity bracelet around my wrist, takes my blood pressure and checks the baby's heartbeat. 'Relaxed and comfortable. Now, where's your birth plan?'

It is the dog-ate-my-homework moment.

'I haven't actually finished it.'

'Sometimes it's better that way. We'll just take it as it comes.'

All those months of anxiety about birth plans, and I never needed worry! I feel a great surge of relief; everything should now be easy. Nicholas slips a Mozart piano concerto into the CD player, and I lie down with my book, ready to begin my holiday. Then I am seized by a contraction and forced to stand up, leaning on Nicholas as he counts me through to its crest, and then back down again.

'Would it help if I caressed your breasts?' he asks.

I laugh, congratulating myself on maintaining a sense of humour.

A midwife bustles in with a basket marked *post-partum haemorrhage*. 'Just covering all the bases,' she explains, when she sees me looking. 'We've been told that you're an *interesting patient*.'

A contraction veers back at me, and I fold myself into Nicholas and breathe through it. Then it vanishes whence it came, and there is a different nurse in the room, demanding I fill out a menu.

'I don't actually have a pen.'

She purses her lips. 'You'd be amazed at how many women present at labour without a pen. You'll just have to source one from somewhere.'

The next contraction lifts me out of this room and out of this problem, and when I come back, the nurse has gone.

'We need to source a pen,' I tell Nicholas.

'Just concentrate on sourcing that baby,' he says.

Baba calls: 'I'm in a taxi.' You and she are converging on this room, but I hope she arrives first. Another contraction, and then immediately another. Humour has vanished now, and I grasp my book like an anchor. Monica arrives for a quick check-up. 'You're doing well! Already five centimetres.'

I turn my TENS machine up to its highest setting, a mini-electrocution that delicately burns my skin, but the next contraction drowns out the sensation. Your Grandma Mariah arrives and I immerse myself further in my book.

She had only one ally in all this, and that was the distant authority of my father. Increasingly, she would remind me of his story, how he had grown up poor, in a poor country, in a poor continent; how his life had been hard ...

The next wave is symphonic, arriving from all directions at once. It takes me out of my body – *out out out* – or so far into it that I no longer know myself – until I see the fissures in the air and feel the lurch of nausea and realise I am returning to the room. Then it vanishes, leaving no residue except a glaze of perspiration on my skin.

'That was outrageous,' I report, returning to my book. It is critical that I better understand the character of Obama's father.

He had led his life according to principles that demanded a different kind of toughness, principles that promised a higher form of power. I would follow his example, my mother decided. I had no choice. It was in the genes …

Two midwives come into the room as the pain swerves back. Forget humour: it is not possible to retain even a sense of self during a contraction. I realise that my job, my only job, is to *bear* it. This is why women are said to bear children.

Someone is groaning. It takes some time to recognise it is me.

'Are the walls soundproof?' I ask.

'Not really,' says the younger one with the pixie haircut.

'Absolutely,' insists the blonde.

Now the contractions come on top of each other, in waves that do not wait until the previous waves have retreated, causing rips and whirlpools and eddies. Surely there must be some upper limit, some ultimate point of unbearability? Or is the body's register of pain infinite? I cling to Nicholas's hand, but it cannot save me.

'This is ridiculous!' I taste salt water in my mouth, and discover I am crying. 'I want it to stop.'

'You're doing so well,' says the midwife. 'And such a good idea to save any pain relief until later, when the contractions get painful.'

Later? When the contractions get painful?

That is the limit for me, the moment of surrender. 'I need gas.'

She fetches the mask, and I ignore her explanations and warnings and plant it on my face, inhaling deeply to make it rattle. It makes no difference. I breathe in greedily, trying to vacuum it into my lungs, fill myself with oblivion. But the pain continues to whirl through me until I have no identity beyond pain. As I listen to the howl of my breath or the howl of my sobbing, I wonder if this gas is a placebo, to give me something to do in front of this awful impotence, to restore the tiniest part of me to myself as a *doing* animal.

The pain expands further to incorporate a new pressure in my pelvis, a type of compulsion. 'I need to push.'

The midwife investigates. 'Oh my.'

There is a flurry of activity.

'I don't think you should push just yet.'

'Because Monica isn't here?'

'This and that. There's a few things to consider.'

'Your lovely little baby will be here soon,' somebody volunteers, but I am in no mood for lovely little babies. I only want this to be over. Then the door swings open, and Baba charges in with her carry-on baggage, and you are free to be born.

Monica arrives immediately behind her, pulling on a pair of latex gloves. 'Take a deep breath over a count of three and then push.'

Somehow, I had believed that pushing was the easy bit, the downward slope after the hard work of contractions. Now, as I push away from pain and deeper into pain, I am shocked by the continued difficulty. It is a pain maze from which there is no exit.

'Take another deep breath and give me an even bigger push,' says Monica.

I hear new sounds from my body, bellows and roars and whimpers, sounds that I did not know I could make. There is nothing left of me to mediate between these sounds and their production – they are as involuntary as a cough, a scream – and yet some part of me eavesdrops, fascinated by this series of possessions. Tigress, child, earth mother: what other selves are here?

A nurse offers me a hand mirror.

'TAKE IT AWAY!'

It is so hard to get you out. I feel I might push the organs of my body out first, through my skin.

'You're doing very well,' says Monica.

I push further, ripping my own body apart. The violence of this! Why have we kept doing this – do we never learn?

'Stay in the moment,' says Monica. 'You're nearly there. Now you just need to get around this corner.'

I stop pushing in protest. *What corner?*

Everybody laughs, the fuckers, and I summon up all my fury and desperation and hope and push to get you around this corner that nobody has ever told me about before and there is a great burning and a gasp from the room and a sweet slithering riddance and *It's a boy* and they put you on my stomach and I stare at you, plump and lobster red, and what does this have to do with anything—

NEW

BEHOLD A SON

—There is a bawling baby on my stomach, furious at being born. Around me, other people are weeping too, but more recreationally. Mine are the only dry eyes here. I know certain responses are expected, certain lines required from the overjoyed mother, but I cannot find my way to them. Instead I am stuck on this non-sequitur: the violence, and now this stranger in the room. The nurse wraps the baby in a blanket and places him on my chest, and I give him a polite pat. He might not yet belong to me, but it is important to make him welcome. Around us there is the iron-rich smell of blood, and something loamy, the smell of new life. Monica fiddles with the wound between my legs, delivering a placenta, performing some sort of needlework. *That's right, just let the baby nuzzle up to you.* He butts at my nipple and turns away. *Don't worry. It gets easier with practice.* But I have no interest in practice, in further learning curves. I have given birth and plan now to retire from all human endeavour. Aunts and cousins and in-laws file into the room. *Our little Par-trick. How about*

Percy? Percy Purcell! I don't think they've decided on a name. I think they're havin' us on! You think they're having a son? I can no longer tell the difference between things that are jokes and things that are not jokes. The nurse confiscates the baby and lowers him on to the scales. *Got your cameras ready for the weigh-in?* Against the silver of the tray he is plump and ruddy as a Christmas ham. A furious Christmas ham. Nicholas leans forward and whispers something in his ear. It is his first proper act as father and full of quiet hope, but now the baby starts bellowing on inhalation as well as exhalation, like a piano accordion. *Look at the giant genitals baby boys have! Do you remember the first time you saw Daniel as a baby? You grabbed yourself between the legs and asked WHERE'S MINE?* No, I do not remember. I was not even two years old, and if Baba were a true feminist, she would stop telling that story. Somewhere a Mozart concerto is still playing, as though labour has never stopped. I turn on my side, away from all these people. I am afraid to sleep, in case I wake and discover I have not yet given birth. But sleep steals over me regardless, and I surrender, my body still bracing itself for the next contraction.

*

When I wake up, I have a baby. And not just any baby. This baby. You.

Your black hair is plastered down with effort, with the labour of being born. Even so, you exude gravitas. How stoical you are. How you shame me with your equilibrium! You, who have had to deal with so much more than me. Not just birth, but its sequel: brand-new life. Your eyes are clenched shut; you sing softly to yourself, still inhabiting the dream-life of the womb. I thought you were getting ahead of yourself, knocking on that door to come out early, but perhaps you knew best. You are clearly a match, more than a match, for all this.

Your Uncle Daniel calls from London. He is due to go in for surgery soon, and I hear his weariness through the fog of my own: 'Nice one, sis. Have you thought about a name?'

As I gaze at you I realise that I know your name. It is not the name that I expected; I hope that Nicholas knows it too.

When the nurse suggests I have a shower, I surrender you to your new family. In the bathroom, I dance in the shower, a child again in my remembered body. Blood swirls around me in a festive pink. 'It's a slasher film,' says Nicholas, and my vacated belly jiggles before me with laughter. How did I never previously know my own lightness? Afterwards I brush my teeth, using the same blue toothbrush as twelve hours before. But in the other room, there is this most marvellous thing. You. Our son. How immediately you occupy that space, how completely you claim ownership of that word.

After the visitors leave, we move into the post-natal ward, where we place you in your bassinet to sleep, and cram into the narrow bed beside you. Sometime around midnight your breath catches for a moment, and Nicholas springs over me in a single bound. I join him at the side of your bassinet, and we listen to your snuffling, your nightingale sounds, your busy midnight baby work, until we are reassured that you will continue breathing. Even so, we stay awhile longer, pointing you out to each other. The immaculate craft of your fingers. Your haughty upper lip; your recessive chin. Of course human life must be expensive. Of course it must come at such a price.

'What should we call him?' I ask Nicholas, shyly.

What is it to name someone? It is a type of creation: a story, a poem.

He tells me, and it is the name I knew you were, too. The name your devout Methodist great-great-grandparents chose for the blessed surprise of their firstborn, your great-grandfather: behold, a son.

MILK

When Sash arrives from Adelaide, she enters the room airborne, seizing you from my lap and sobbing into your face. You open a single eye to register the phenomenon of *aunt* and then fall back to sleep.

'Do you love him?' she asks.

My whole body is steeped in your smell, each of my cells suffused with your sweetness, your obliviousness. I even feel tender towards the smells of my own body – the lochia, the residual amniotic fluids – because they remind me of you, of your birth. Already it has become a magnificent experience. Already it is something I would not trade.

'Of course I love him.'

When you start crying, Nicholas swoops in, new expert of the swaddle. He spreads the muslin carefully on the bed, lays you in its centre and performs a delicate origami. Then he passes you to me, neat as a rice-paper roll.

'Has your milk come in?' asks Sash.

'You make it sound like a weather condition.'

I park you at my breast and you turn away.

'You'd better say something to the nurses if it hasn't.'

But I will not admit failure so early in my new career. I want to succeed at motherhood. And anyway, you seem content without milk, dining still on the fat of the womb.

The paediatrician sticks her head around the door. 'Is this a good time?'

'A very good time,' Sash says. 'We have lots to ask you.'

'He's a very easy baby,' I tell her. 'Sleeping through the night already.'

As she examines you, a slideshow of expressions flickers across your face, rehearsals for your emotional life: joy, derision, wonder. After you have moved through the known expressions, you continue to improvise: a furrowed brow with puckered mouth; a gummy snarl with lopsided wink.

'Aren't you a beautiful, perfect boy?' the doctor gushes, obligingly. 'Now, what did you want to ask?'

'Nothing.' I avoid Sash's eye.

'How's the breastfeeding going?'

'Fine.' I put you to my breast and you snuggle in tight and she leaves. We are good fakers, you and I.

Nicholas's family has graciously retreated for the weekend, ceding the territory to interstate guests. When Baba returns at lunch-time, Sash takes out her watch. 'I'm not even taking into account the entire *bonus afternoon* of cuddles you had yesterday.

But since I'm the one flying out tonight, I insist on fairness. You have seventeen minutes left. Don't waste them.'

'You're a hard, hard woman,' Baba says, and I settle back into my narcoleptic cloud of you-smell. As I close my eyes, your different faces flick through my mind like a pack of cards. I wake to find Sash cradling you in the armchair, and Baba drumming her fingers on the windowpane.

'What's wrong, Mum?'

'Daniel called,' she sighs. 'Looks like he's going into hospital on Wednesday, to get that poxy lung fixed.'

I meet Sash's eye and form a coalition. 'That's good news.'

'It's great news,' Sash agrees. 'It's a routine operation. He had the other lung fixed with no complications, and now he'll be able to fly again.'

'I don't like two of my children being in hospital at the same time. I just don't like it, *not one bit*.'

'Look at this!' Sash props you up on her hand, your cheeks pink with effort. There is a muffled grunt and then the faint dawning of a smile.

Baba cheers up immediately. 'That's my boy! Give him to his mother then. She's got to learn how to change him.'

I step up to the change table as to a stage and remove your nappy. The meconium is viscous, sticky as Vegemite, adhering to your tiny sex, to the fingerprint grooves of your scrotum. How am I supposed to get it off? I dab at it gingerly with a nappy wipe.

Sash pushes me aside. 'For God's sake. This is how you change a baby.'

She wipes you clean with three deft strokes and applies another nappy. I do not need to turn around to know that Baba is grinning, that this is a tale that will be retold. For its familiar comedy but also for its reassurance: that despite the week's large upheavals we will each continue to honour our designated roles.

Neither night nor day exists in the small warren of the hospital. Different shades of twilight only, differentiated by the nurses' levels of industry, by the beginning or end of visiting hours. Nurses bustle in and out, administering ice packs, dispensing Panadols. Visitors arrive and then leave, trailing opinions. It is a relief when they have gone, when I no longer have to perform motherhood, and it is just you and me.

On the second evening, a nurse coaches us in your first bath. She demonstrates the preferred hold, hooking her left hand around the back of your neck and lowering you gently into the water.

'Make sure the water is not too hot or too cold. If it's too hot, you might scald him, but if it's too cold, he could get a chill.'

'Concentrate,' I tell Nicholas.

'*You* concentrate.'

'You should both concentrate,' she says sternly.

Underwater, you are slippery and un-muscled, elusive as a fish. Only when you are clothed and swaddled and a solid object once more in my arms do I feel safe. But now another nurse wheels a mobile hearing test through the door. She attaches a set of electrodes to your head and administers a series of small clicks in your ear. You maintain an authoritative, yogic stillness, as if too self-sufficient for sound as well as food.

The nurse furrows her brow. 'If he fails his second test tomorrow, we'll refer you to a specialist.'

I turn to Nicholas as soon as she leaves. 'We'll have to learn sign language!'

'Don't give yourself over to worry.'

'Our poor deaf baby.' My voice becomes resonant with despair. 'Never to know music. Never to know the Mozart he was born to.'

'Snap out of it,' Nicholas says. 'Remember the hypnosis. Move through the wave when it is there, but do not anticipate it.'

Pop arrives that evening with pizza and seizes you from your bassinet: 'My first grandson and heir!'

He lays you down on the change table.

'I just changed him, Dad.'

He ignores me, removing your nappy with a flourish and expertly dabbing on cream.

The nurse smiles at him. 'I think you might have done that before.'

'Riding a bicycle,' he winks.

Afterwards, I follow him outside to the hospital courtyard while he holds you aloft like a trophy: 'My first grandson!' The nurses smile back at him, the warmth of their indulgence lapping against me in his wake, as I struggle with the bassinet and lukewarm pizza.

We sit down on white plastic chairs, and he places you on the table before him for examination.

'He's a lot like you,' I say. It is important that all familial bonds be tightened to their maximum.

He shoots me a canny look. 'You reckon? I think he's just himself.'

You inhale the cool night air and start purring.

'He failed his hearing test this morning,' I say, after a while.

He shrugs. 'That'd just be fluid build-up. Those tests are notoriously unreliable.'

I remember the great relief of being around my father. 'Are you worried about Daniel?'

'Not really. It's a standard procedure. And then he can come home and meet my first grandson.'

As he croons into your face, I do see a familial likeness, or at least I try to. There are specific gifts I would like Pop to bequeath you. His optimism, his trust in his own charm. Entry into his personal universe, a place both rational and benevolent, where things exist to stimulate his curiosity or admire him, or both. My access has always been sporadic, but I hope that you might be able to live there too.

At midnight, something new happens. You wake up and start to scream. Nicholas re-swaddles you according to his latest technique, but it does not help. Your face curls up in fury; your tiny mouth opens wide for the furnace of your cry.

Could this be the soundtrack of our future life?

This time when I bring you to my nipple, you pounce on it like a vampire, clamping it tight between your gums.

'It shouldn't hurt,' insists Nicholas. 'Try again. Nipple to nose, establish latch.'

'I don't need a coach!'

Your suction increases by the second, until you must be drawing blood as well as milk. But at least you are silent. I time my endurance by the digital clock, by its reluctant flicker every long minute. After fifteen minutes, I can bear it no longer and dislodge you with my finger. An angry, red nipple pops out; there is a moment of bewilderment and you are screaming again.

'For God's sake, put him back!' Nicholas dives towards us, a one-man SWAT team, and thrusts you on to the other breast. We have only just established latch when the night nurse steps in on her rounds. 'You certainly seem to be doing well!'

I smile faintly while you tighten your clamp. You have already ruined one nipple: what are we going to do when you have destroyed this one too?

She sits close on the bed beside me, so that I can smell her fragrant hair. 'I just loved breastfeeding. It made me feel so *woman*. Have you considered co-sleeping?'

'Do you recommend it?'

She glances around the room. Her visit has a clandestine, slumber-party feel. 'It's not what they'll tell you here, but yes, absolutely. What's your current parenting strategy?'

My current parenting strategy is to get through this minute and then the one that comes after. But the more you suck, the less feasible this becomes. A single tear escapes my eye and bounces off your cheek.

'Are you okay, sweetheart?'

'It's just a bit painful.'

'Is it actually *painful*, or is it just an unusual sensation?'

'Just an unusual sensation,' I say bitterly. 'Like birth.'

She gazes at me levelly, with earth-mother eyes. 'It's okay to *own your anger*, honey. How would you rate your discomfort, out of ten?'

I stare at her dumbly. My pain meter has recently been recalibrated.

'Come here, little baby boy. Give Mama a break.' She slips her forefinger into your mouth and flinches. 'Ouch! He has the bite of a piranha.'

I feel momentarily gratified that you have such temperament, and that the nurse now has a sore finger. But her pager beeps and she withdraws from the room, abandoning me to my piranha.

By morning, I have been reduced to the three wounds of my groin and breasts, and you are still hungry. A different nurse weighs you and then turns to me outraged. 'Haven't you been feeding him? The poor creature's starving! We're going to have to start him on some formula.' She summons another nurse, who returns with a syringe of formula. After I sign a disclaimer, you glug it down like an orphaned animal and finally fall asleep.

My eyes fill with the fat tears of a failed cow. I have flunked the first test of motherhood, and now we will not be promoted to our hotel mini-break. Even worse: you are not yet three days old and already you have consumed formula. How will you ever recover?

When you wake up, we are sent to the Breastfeeding Room, where three other desolate mothers sit in armchairs, pressing tiny babies like fruit flies against the giant melons of their breasts. Presiding over them, conducting the conveyance of milk, is Lavinia the Lactation Consultant.

'I don't want to keep repeating myself, ladies, but I will if I have to. *Chest to chest, nose to nipple, flick that nipple in!*' She turns to me. 'Sit down and establish latch, and I'll be with you in a minute.'

I sit down and try to establish latch, awaiting condemnation. When Lavinia approaches, she appraises us with the sceptical eye of a professional critic. Then she delivers a grudging nod. 'Ladies, stop what you are doing and observe. A textbook attachment!'

As the other mothers eye me, I feel giddy with triumph. Why should the approval of Lactation Consultants mean so much to me? But then you bite harder, and my grimace gives us away, so that Lavinia leans in to examine your mouth. 'Don't tell me.' She whips you off the breast and sticks her finger under your tongue. '*Another* tongue-tie. This is unbelievable. My *third* for today.'

She pulls out a pad of paper and scribbles something: a fine, perhaps, for tongue-tie infringement. 'Don't say a word to the paediatrician, who will doubtless know better. But that frenulum needs to be snipped as soon as you get out of here. It's preventing him from establishing latch. That's why he's biting.' She passes me the paper, which contains a single name and address, like an abortionist, or bootlegger. 'Time is of the essence. Don't bother with an appointment. As soon as you leave hospital, just turn up and demand he cuts it for you *there and then*. Your milk supply is in peril.'

She places you in your trolley and wheels you into the naughty corner, where you maintain a shamed silence. Then she fetches a large contraption that resembles a vacuum cleaner, and attaches it to my breasts. 'You will express for twenty minutes on the hour, *every* hour, and feed him at least every two hours, with thirty minutes on each breast.'

I perform a dismayed mathematics. 'But that means there's only twenty minutes every two hours in which I'm not producing milk.'

'Correct. Your life is now about milk and nothing else. If need be, I will place a ban on visitors.'

The expressing machine begins its dull, rhythmic wringing, and my bovine transformation is complete. After ninety minutes, I have acquired three millimetres of pale gold at the bottom of the jar, packed with antibodies and nutrients. I have never been so proud of a liquid. My breasts feel spent and virtuous, a pair of athletes after a successful marathon.

Lavinia wheels you back to me. 'Get that into him straightaway.'

I draw the colostrum inside the syringe and drip it into your gasping mouth. There is great satisfaction in administering these crucial nutrients, the elixir of life, and for the first time since your birth I feel properly a mother. Afterwards I place you on my shoulder and pat your back, as I have seen other mothers do. You burp loudly, and dispatch the elixir of life down my back.

BLOOD

Two days later, on a diet of formula and expressed milk, you have regained enough weight. When you pass your second hearing test, we are released from hospital, just as Daniel enters hospital in London. Since arriving, we have acquired a sleuth of teddy bears, a small orchard of flowers, a festival of balloons. We pack this booty into the car, strap you into the throne of your baby capsule and roll down the hill to our home. Cars overtake us, travelling perilously close to the speed limit. I have never before understood *Baby on Board* signs – those boasts of procreation – but now I see their necessity. We should be travelling with a police escort.

As soon as we arrive at the flat, Nicholas unstraps you from your capsule. 'The dog must smell his sock.' He presents your foot to the dog, who sniffs it contemptuously and retreats to his basket. I study your sleepy face for a reaction, but you remain inscrutable.

Baba has scrubbed the kitchen clean and piled your presents in a pyramid on the dining table. 'Are you going to open your presents or what?' she asks.

There is something overwhelming about them: the human clamour they represent, the obligation. 'We might have a nap first.'

She grinds her teeth. 'Whatever you want.'

It takes me a moment to register her anxiety. 'What's wrong?'

She sighs. 'I'm just not happy about Daniel having an operation on the other side of the world. I just *don't like it*.'

'He'll be fine, Mum. It's a routine operation, and he's had it before.'

'Off you go, then, you *couple of sloths*. I'll look after the baby.'

Some time later, we are awoken by a commotion in the kitchen. I emerge to find Baba rearranging the cutlery drawer. 'The operation should be over by now, but Mutale hasn't called.'

I fish around for some stray wisdom and Vera springs to mind, improbable as a fairy godmother. 'Move through the wave when it is there, but do not anticipate it.'

She snorts and returns to the cutlery. When you wake bawling, I take you to the cane chair near the window, and feed you until it becomes unbearable.

Baba sticks her finger under your tongue. 'We need to get this tongue-tie sorted out, and pronto.'

'What should we do?'

'Avoid unnecessary operations at any cost.' She leans over and scrutinises my bleeding nipple. 'But this is beyond the pale. We'll get him fixed today.'

Her phone rings, and she fishes it out of her handbag. There is a moment's silence, and then she catapults it across the table. 'I knew it.'

'What happened?'

'They've taken him back into theatre.' She speaks on the inward gasp, as though choking on her own words. 'They can't stop him bleeding.'

But Daniel is the physically competent one, the one who is able to do things. He can play seven instruments; he can dribble a soccer ball with a dancer's grace; he can juggle four balls with one hand. Daniel is the one with the reliable body; surely it would not betray him like this.

'He's in the best hospital in London,' I falter. Could the universe really be so heavy-handed with its mathematics? With you only five days old? Have we been too greedy, wanting to love in so many directions at once? You start screaming, and Nicholas swaddles you and then turns you on your side. He jiggles your head gently with one finger, but it does not help.

Baba goes into the other room to call Pop, and I can hear her professional, problem-solving voice through the wall. 'Yes, the haematologist had advised clotting agents …'

When she comes back, she seizes her keys from the table and lurches towards the front door. 'Come on then.'

'Where are we going?'

'To fix this boy.'

'Are you sure?'

'No point sitting around here doing nothing.'

Her head juts forward; there is a heaviness to the way she pushes herself through air. Nicholas hands you to me, and I hurry after her down the hall.

Outside the hospital, I wrap you in three blankets before removing you from your capsule. This is your first proper excursion, and in the outside light you are newer than ever.

'How old?' gasps a woman walking past.

'Five days.' For a moment, pride displaces anxiety about Daniel. As if your newness were your achievement, or my own.

Ahead of us, Baba stalks into the consulting rooms, where a secretary glances up from a magazine. 'I'm sorry. The doctor is completely booked.'

'We were sent by Lavinia the Lactation Consultant,' I announce, significantly.

The girl shrugs and returns to her magazine, but then Baba leans in, enunciating her words. '*Listen to me.* I appreciate that the doctor is busy. But this is an emergency. *The baby is not drinking.*'

The secretary hesitates, before tapping her keyboard with one finger. 'I can't promise anything, but if you take a seat he might be able to squeeze you in later.'

We sit down in the waiting room and begin waiting – for the doctor to call us in, for Baba's phone to ring – until I wonder if we have somehow sought this room out, for our waiting. At least I have a job through this: I am a milk-producing animal. Beside me, Baba remains straight-backed, refusing to surrender to the sofa's comfort. Her knuckles are white against her phone; every few minutes, she checks to see that it is still turned on.

'Maybe you should get on the next plane to London,' I suggest.

'And be out of contact for fourteen hours?'

On the sofa in the corner, a woman feeds a baby from a bottle; her husband sits beside them, typing on a laptop. They shine with the patina of prosperity, of good fortune, but when she turns the baby around I see that he has a cleft palate. The phone rings and you jerk awake. Baba hesitates a moment before answering it. It is Mutale, reporting that Daniel is still in theatre, that she will call as soon as she hears anything further. The doctor saunters out and greets the couple. They talk about tennis and then retreat into his room, laughing.

You have only just fallen back to sleep when the phone rings again. Baba's voice is low and authoritative. 'Thank you. I know you are.' She hangs up. 'That was the surgeon. He says he's doing everything he would do for his own son.'

'Was he nice?'

'Seemed nice. Good of him to call.'

Daniel has a nice surgeon looking after him in London. It is no consolation. I hand you to Baba so that I can go into an empty consulting room to express milk. If I can fill this tiny jar right up to the top, perhaps Daniel will be okay. The milk drips out reluctantly; my useless tears flow freely. I look away as I work, so as not to be discouraged. After fifteen minutes, I swap hands to relieve the cramp in my thumb, and then swap back again. When I have finished, I fasten the lid on tightly, place the warm jar in my pocket and return to the waiting room.

'I filled up the jar.'

'That's great news,' Baba says faintly.

The doctor wears a bow-tie, and bright irreverent glasses. 'I snip at least fifty of these a year and have never had any complications.' He leans back in his chair, folding his arms behind his head. 'A simple cut to the frenulum and at this age they heal immediately. Any existing conditions?'

Baba clears her throat. 'There is a bleeding disorder in the family.'

My nipples administer a warning prick under my shirt. 'The birth was fine,' I reassure him. 'No complications. And we have no reason to think the baby has the disorder.'

'Thrombocytopenia?'

'Portsmouth Syndrome,' Baba says. 'Impaired platelet function rather than count.'

He removes his feet from the desk in a single deft gesture. 'How have other family members responded to surgery?'

I look at Baba hopelessly. She glares at the surgeon. Of course we were never going to be able to fix you.

'My son's in theatre in London right now.' She spits the words out as if this were the doctor's doing, as if he were part of a worldwide conspiracy of surgeons. *And they can't stop him bleeding.*

There is silence in the room, then the doctor stands to show us to the door. 'I'm very sorry to hear about your son, ma'am.

But you understand that I cannot help you.'

Back at home, restored to impotence, we sit in the living room and stare at cups of tea. When they get cold, Nicholas takes them away and makes new ones. I rotate the way I feed you, from the cradle hold, to the footballer's hold, to the inverted cradle. But you are still hungry and frustrated. You are still failing to thrive. And your uncle is still bleeding.

Mutale calls to say they have taken Daniel back to surgery for a fourth procedure, and then calls to say he is still there. I come to despise Baba's ringtone, its facetious cheer. When Mutale calls to say they were unable to wake him, and have taken him back in for a fifth time, I go into the other room to phone Pop, seeking the reassurance of his world view.

'I still think he might be okay,' he says huskily. 'But if he pulls through, I'll start going to church.'

After I hang up, I call Sash.

'I'll be on the next plane,' she says.

It has been twelve hours since we came home to begin our new life, since Daniel went into theatre. You are now refusing to drink even from your syringe. Baba sits at the table in silence, drowning in mother love. It is so enormous, so elemental, that I can scarcely look at it, scarcely acknowledge its existence in this flat. I am still learning to manage my own. Nicholas cooks pasta for dinner. Nobody eats, but Baba tells me I have to. As I am forking it into my mouth, I feel her ringtone as a shock on my skin the moment before I hear it. She listens and then hangs up.

Her teeth clank together like a skeleton's; she spills her tea across the table.

'That was the surgeon. He says he has run out of ideas.' Nicholas fetches her a heat pack, and I wrap her in a nest of blankets. For once she does not resist our care.

Several hours later, Sash arrives and takes Baba into the room across the hall. We go to bed and wait some more. For you to start crying. For Baba to come back. Every two hours, I get up and feed you. In several months, perhaps, your mouth will be big enough that feeding no longer hurts, but now I just wait for each feed to be over.

At midnight, Baba has still not returned. No news can only be good news, in the ongoing provisional present. You finish drinking and I burp you, then prop you in front of me to study you, to fix this moment in time. This moment in which you are not crying. This moment in which you are still a newborn, in which Daniel is still with us. There is a filigree of veins across your temple, the slightest hint of blue in the whites of your eyes. When I take your leg in my hand, your thigh bone is a twig between my fingers, and I feel your vulnerability to the point of pity. Across the hall, Baba lies awake, grasping her phone. Her innocence presses in on me, and our own. What were we thinking, to take this on?

An hour later, Baba receives a final call. Then she makes another call in which she says hardly anything at all. And your two estranged grandparents are joined in that silence, as they weep together over the phone line. Because early this morning, your uncle stopped bleeding for no reason at all. Because death, on a whim, passed by this family tonight and we are safe again, until the next contraction.

WORMHOLES

Now that you have been here for two weeks, you are becoming worldly. Every day you reveal new accomplishments:

That pleased noise you make after you sneeze: 'Ahhh.' I am not sure what it says about you, but it must be something special.

Your quick karate chops, spasmodic and strobe-lit.

Your graceful arm movements as you listen to Mozart. 'Come and look – the baby's conducting!'

Nicholas grabs the video camera and films until the end of the movement. Later we will upload this video to a blog, hiding behind self-satire, hoping our friends will recognise your giftedness anyway. But there are certain things that give us away.

My whisper: 'Look how he brings in the orchestra after the cadenza!'

Our awed laughter.

Loving you is like having a crush on a celebrity – wholly one-sided – and yet your dependence on us is absolute. One evening you start screaming in your cot, and we cast off your blankets in search of an assailant. Your scream becomes louder, and our search more desperate, until Nicholas notices you are pulling your own hair. The more it hurts, the more fiercely you yank; there is no communication between hand and hair, no acknowledgement of shared provenance. Nicholas holds you still as I prise open your grip. Afterwards you sob on my chest, self-molested.

As you become more human, I become more animal. When you wake at night, my arms register your cry before my ears do: a muscular alarm, an anticipated fatigue. In the morning, I love you with the rock hardness of my breasts, a tingling behind the nipples that is a type of desire. Even in my sleep, I keep one ear focused on your snuffling breath in the adjoining room. Sometimes it catches for a moment and instantly I am standing at the side of your cot, praying for the safe passage of air through your windpipe. A windpipe that could be blocked by a large speck of dust; a windpipe through which all future happiness must first pass. Nicholas buys a sensor, and we position its blinking green light in view of our bed. It is a light that tells us you are still breathing, but which I come to believe makes you breathe.

At three weeks, it is time for our first family outing. The pageantry is extravagant: the new super-pusher Baba gave us, with mosquito net, rain cover and upholstery options; a selection of blankets for all possible weather conditions; a nappy bag that has been packed, unpacked and repacked according to various lists found on the internet. I scoop my liquid components into clothes, and we venture out as a caravan, with Nicholas, Baba and the dog.

As we walk to the café, I smile at each pedestrian we pass with a type of noblesse oblige, granting them permission to compliment you.

'Beautiful day,' offers a power-walker, and continues her power-walking.

Next to the cemetery, a middle-aged woman stops with a shriek of appreciation: 'That is a gorgeous dog!'

Baba shakes her head at me. As we arrive at the café, a bearded man races across the road to intercept us. 'Sorry to interrupt, but my girlfriend wants to know, what sort of dog is that?'

'A spoodle,' I tell him, frostily.

'Are these people blind, or what?' Baba asks, and the dog wags his tail, vindicated.

A waitress guides us to a table, where I tilt you towards the morning sun and you sneeze and then say 'Ahhh.'

'He always makes that remark,' I explain.

After breakfast, I leave Nicholas and Baba at the café and push you down the street to the Family Health Centre. It is our maiden solo voyage, and before crossing the road I glance back at base camp. Baba grips the sides of the table. 'Be careful!' she mouths. We succeed in crossing the road, and step through the automated glass doors into the health centre, where a woman is cooing over a baby girl.

'How old is she?' I ask.

'Two weeks.'

I remember those days well, but they cannot really compare to the riches of three weeks. 'She's very sweet.'

'Your baby's sweet too,' she says, without looking. 'But you would not believe Bridie's temperament. I tell you: we're going to have our hands full!'

Bridie gazes towards me and her eyes swivel to the side. There is something amusing about this mother's projections: the distinction she confers on this endearing blob, as formless as a Tamagotchi.

'Look at the way she's pointing – so feisty! It's *exactly* my Aunt Virginia.'

I wait for her to finish talking, so that I can describe your more clearly defined character – the way you conduct Mozart, the noise you make after you sneeze – but the nurse calls us into her room before the opportunity arrives.

'Hello there, Mummy. I'm Nurse Fran. First of all, how are you?'

Isn't it obvious? I even applied lipstick this morning. 'Very well, thank you.'

'Are you feeling anxious?'

There is a mobile of farmyard animals dangling above the examination table, which might fall down and hit you in the face. But it is only paper, so it would not hurt. Unless it administered a paper cut to your eye, or lodged in your mouth and choked you.

'No more than usual.'

She stares at me for a moment longer than is comfortable. 'Take his clothes off and put him on the table. Hello, Mister, aren't you just a gorgeous boy?' As she weighs and measures you, making appreciative noises, I realise she is an excellent nurse. You gurgle and then start to hiccup and she leans in to examine your torso. 'Looks like he's got a paradoxical chest wall.'

'A what?'

'See how his chest dips when he hiccups? It should correct itself in time. Oh yes, and what do we have down here?' She wiggles her fingers into your belly button. 'A small umbilical hernia.'

I have read somewhere that the average baby is born with three birth defects. Surely, added to your tongue-tie, this is your quota filled, small defects to keep the larger ones at bay. They are distinguished, polysyllabic ailments — *a paradoxical chest wall, an umbilical hernia* — the sort of thing I can drop into conversation next time I meet another mother, as further proof of your distinction.

'What exactly is an umbilical hernia?'

'Nothing to worry about, really. It just means the wall of his abdomen is not completely formed. But if his intestines start to fall out of his navel, you'll need to take him to Emergency. Obviously.'

Nothing to worry about, really, but now I will check your belly button every hour, even when you are asleep. There are fissures everywhere, I realise, wormholes through which you could slip if I am not vigilant. *Do not look at or even think about your baby's fontanels*, Sash has warned me. Now, when you hiccup, I pull up your singlet and watch your ribcage jab back towards your spine, in a giant concave V. It is a V for vortex, for the void that seeks to reclaim you. I must remain awake to ensure that it does not.

*

After several weeks of sleeplessness, Nicholas and I are no longer comrades-in-arms. We have reached the limit of our generosity towards each other: those ten minutes of extra rest. If Nicholas takes an unauthorised nap during the day, my housework becomes loud and punitive. Some nights, your breath is peaceful, and we plunge together into sleep, direct as deep-sea divers. But when you wake, we each remain still a moment longer than necessary, hoping the other will stir.

One night, you free yourself from your swaddle and do battle with your face, engraving your skin with the fine stylus of your fingernail. In the morning, I try to gnaw your fingernails down, but they are too small for my teeth.

'Be careful, there!' warns Grandma Mariah, as I steer the nail scissors around the pale crescent of your thumb. It is painstaking work, a type of microsurgery. When I arrive at your ring finger, you jerk away from me, and I nip the skin. There is a moment before you scream, a moment in which to register that drop of blood, inflammatory red, against the white of your muslin.

So it is there after all, just as I suspected.

ABdlessly, Mariah takes you from me, staunching your tiny wound with a snippet of band-aid. Then she makes me a cup of tea to sip until I stop shaking.

The following week it is time for your first immunisations. We drive to the local town hall, take a number and sit in the waiting room. Loud screams issue from the next room: the room in which people put needles in children. A volunteer ushers us into a row of chairs against the back wall, so that we can watch the other babies being injected. It is the same scenario, re-enacted: the trusting child, curled into its mother; the mother's perusal of the checklist and reluctant nod; the baby's octaves of outrage; the tearful dyad retreating from the room. And the nurses becoming jollier with every jab. You lie on my lap, oblivious, but the two-year-old girl beside us starts trembling.

A cheerful nurse summons us to the front. She blows some bubbles, and you smile complacently. Then I offer up your fat thigh, and she plunges the needle in. There is a moment of shock, of bodily confusion. *This cannot be happening.* But then, even as you protest, I offer up your second thigh. This is the unforgivable transgression: the second insult, in full knowledge of the first.

Your scream now carries a note of accusation, but it is not this that undoes me. It is that I have bred a body with pain receptors, a body designed to receive pain. Pain that I feel twice as keenly as my own, in a body over which I have only remote control. I apply you to the breast and you suck until you forget, but I cannot.

COMPOSTING TOILET

By February we need a holiday, so Nicholas books a farmhouse near the coast. We abandon our steaming flat at the beginning of a heatwave and speed down the ocean road like fugitives. Ahead of us, the sea and sky merge into a holiday blue. It is the kind of blue that would previously have induced feelings of wellbeing; there is surely nostalgic value in this.

'Did you pack the sensor?'

'Bugger.' Nicholas slows the car. 'What shall we do?'

Babies have survived for millennia without sensors. On the other hand, some have not. What if you chose to stop breathing during the week we forgot your sensor? But that would be so coincidental as to be cosmic malevolence.

I hesitate. 'Keep going.'

He rests his hand on my leg for a moment and we are again allies. That old holiday promise of renewal: that we can go on a holiday from sleep deprivation, from hyper-vigilance. That we can go on a holiday from ourselves.

As the day warms up, the beaches empty out and the car's air-conditioning begins to struggle. In my mind, I rehearse the necessary manoeuvres were the car to skid off the road into the ocean, the exact choreography of seatbelt removal and window unwinding. Every hour we stop to hydrate you, so it is late afternoon by the time we arrive at the dirt track up to the house.

'Careful,' I say, as the car pants up the hill.

'Careful is my default mode.'

'Careful,' I whisper when we turn.

'Can you please stop saying that?'

But I cannot. At every corner, the word slips out of my mouth, involuntary as breathing. The track narrows to a single lane, and dirt fills the air. Three hot sheep wander into the middle of the road to stare grimly into the car. Nicholas toots the horn, and they canter off with surprising grace.

'It's a long way from the town,' I observe.

'It'll be worth it,' he says, as we grind further up the hill.

When we arrive, I see that he is right. The house is spacious, immaculate as a magazine spread, with light flooding in from all sides. There are wide decks, forest vistas, smooth linen and fine crockery, and a large table of distressed wood on which I can write. It is a holiday house that promises everything, including the opportunity to reclaim myself.

'Why was it such a bargain?'

Nicholas takes out his camera to document the house, to confirm its existence. 'No idea.'

I feed and change you, as the dog rushes outside to caper on the lawns. Afterwards I place you on the day bed by the window, where you make celebratory noises and then abruptly fall asleep.

'Odd that there's no air-conditioning,' Nicholas says, coming in from the deck.

'Once we open it up there'll be a gully breeze.'

'A gully breeze on *top* of a hill?'

I move through the house, flinging doors and windows open. 'Of course.'

It is only when I go to the toilet that I discover a flaw in this paradise. *This is a composting toilet. Please drop in a scoop of sawdust mixture after every use.* I open the lid to an underground sea of shit, yawning back at me, moist and malodorous. Afterwards there is not the closure of a flush, only a scoop of sawdust into its greedy maw. Quickly I close the lid, but it is too late. I have seen how you would fall. That moment in which clumsiness ticks over into disaster. The dense plummet of your body; the viscous splash. The too-small hole, through which I could never follow you. It is yet another of these vortices, these sinkholes, and even after I have run from the room and slammed the door I feel its sinister gravitational pull.

'What's wrong?' asks Nicholas, jiggling you on his lap in the living room.

'There's a long-drop toilet!'

He stands to investigate, and I snatch you from his arms. '*The baby must never go in there!*'

I take you into the dining room and close the door.

'I don't think you should be scared of the toilet,' he says, coming in.

'What if the baby fell in?'

'How would he get in there? He's incapable of locomotion.'

'One of us might take him in.'

'So we won't take him in.'

But our holiday house has been exposed as a fraud, as a front for the composting toilet with its macabre appetites. In the kitchen, the thermometer rises to forty-five degrees, and the dog unravels another inch of pink tongue. At dusk, a plague of insects descends upon the house, and we run from room to room closing windows, so that they thud against the glass. I put you to bed and we sit down to watch *The Sopranos*. There is still no sign of a gully breeze. Always I am aware of the composting toilet, of its patient waiting. It is too hot to be awake, and when we go to bed it is too hot to be asleep. Even lying naked is an exertion. Nicholas falls asleep regardless, while my heart rate accelerates. I try to slow it with logic.

You are incapable of locomotion.

The only people capable of taking you into the composting toilet are me and Nicholas.

I repeat these statements in my head as though counting sheep.

You are incapable of locomotion.

The only people capable of taking you into the composting toilet are me and Nicholas.

I will not take you into the composting toilet.

Therefore, the person who will take you into the composting toilet is Nicholas.

I knew it! It is incontestable as a mathematical proof, but I turn it around further in my head, searching for fallacies.

Even though Nicholas has said he will not take you in, he does not properly appreciate the threat.

There is a danger that he will forget and take you anyway, and then accidentally drop you in.

And there is the additional danger that he might take you in his sleep.

It is important that I remain awake to prevent this.

But if I stay awake now I might fall asleep tomorrow, leaving you alone with Nicholas and at greater risk.

I get out of bed and arrange a small pile of suitcases by his side of the bed, so that if he gets up in the night he will trip and alert me. Then I climb back into bed and wrap my arms about him, my leaking breasts adhering to his back.

'It's too hot.' He tries to shake me off, but I clasp my hands more tightly until his body slackens with sleep.

You are incapable of locomotion.

The only people capable of taking you into the composting toilet are me and Nicholas.

'Ra!' you shout from the other room, and I jump up to feed you. There is a relief in rehydrating you, and in knowing that when you are in my arms you are not in the composting toilet. Afterwards, I place you back in your bassinet, check that the toilet door is still closed, and return to bed.

I will not take you into the composting toilet.

Therefore, the person who will take you into the composting toilet is Nicholas.

Sometime around midnight a baby mouse scurries into the room and I shoot it with my hunting gun. Why did I have to do this? Who would have thought a small mouse could contain so much blood?

'What's wrong?' Nicholas asks.

'I just had the most terrible nightmare.'

He turns over. 'What happened?'

I can scarcely talk through disorientation and terror. 'I dreamt that I *shot a mouse.*'

For a moment he is still, but then his belly trembles with laughter, and he heaves himself up in bed.

'Where are you going?'

'To the toilet.'

Before he has climbed out of bed, I have rushed to your room to stand sentry at your door. There is a loud thud from the master bedroom: 'What the fuck?'

'Just checking on the baby,' I explain, as he limps by.

I am still loitering by your door when he returns. 'There's something you should know,' he says, taking my hands in his. 'I'm not planning to take the baby out of bed in order to drop him down the composting toilet.'

'Shhh! I never thought you were.'

We return to bed, where he falls asleep and I resume my calculations.

The only people capable of taking you into the composting toilet are me and Nicholas.

I will not take you into the composting toilet.

I sense a flaw in my logic, the dawning of a new possibility.

What if I were to carry you there in my sleep?

This is a knight's move: checkmate. If I cannot trust myself with you, whom can I trust? Tears form in my eyes and dry immediately in the heat; my pulse thuds in my ears. As I lie there, paralysed by fear of myself, another sound starts in cross-rhythm, a sound that part of me always knew was coming: the urgent squeal of the smoke alarm.

Nicholas dashes to the kitchen; I run to your bedroom, where you are still sleeping. As he surveys the laundry and living spaces, I check the composting toilet for signs of spontaneous combustion, and then follow him outside into the black clamour of the forest.

We sniff the air like dogs. 'Can you smell smoke?'

'Only eucalyptus,' he says. 'The heat must have set off the alarm. I'd better disable it.'

'Disable a smoke alarm in a forest cottage in the middle of a heatwave?'

'There's still the others.'

We return inside where he prods the alarm with a broom handle and then goes back to bed. I am staggered by how much we have grown apart over the course of this holiday. How can he even think about sleep? At least the composting toilet is local in its threat. What chance would we have against bushfire, isolated on top of a hill? I patrol the house, naked and sniffing, detached from humanity by fear. Within ten minutes, another smoke alarm starts up in the laundry. Then immediately, half a semitone flatter, an alarm in the living room. Nicholas rushes out to join me.

'Are we going crazy?' he asks. 'Nothing's burning.'

'Why would all the alarms be going off if nothing's burning?'

'It's forty-six degrees in here. They must be cracking up from the heat.'

This time you wake bawling and I take you out to the deck, as Nicholas disables the alarms, our last line of defence. Out here, the air is thick as water; the forest crackles like kindling. I place you on my breast to extinguish your cry. You doze off, but I continue to hold you, scanning the horizon for the glow of flame. I do not wish to return inside, into that parody of shelter.

If I am holding you, I can monitor you for signs of dehydration.

If I am holding you, Nicholas cannot drop you in the composting toilet.

If I remain awake, I will not be surprised by fire.

I sit and wait, held taut by my triangulated fears. How foolish to imagine we could escape the heat, or exhaustion, or our anxiety.

Beneath my palm I feel the busy work of your digestion, and I glance down at the great dome of your sleeping head, at your champignon nose, at the beak of your upper lip. Bringing a child into this world is exposing it to danger. I thought I understood this, that I had read the fine print; blithely I signed my name on the dotted line. But not being able to keep you safe is intolerable. Even if I succeed in shielding you from bushfire, from composting toilets, from intestinal spillage, from all the wormholes of daily existence, both natural and manmade, there is still the danger that you might suddenly die in the night for *no reason at all*. What cosmic sadist invents such a system, designed to torment parents, and then throws sleep deprivation into the mix? And even if we manage to duck and weave the perils of infanthood, then childhood and adolescence, and make it through to adulthood – who is to say you will not move to London and be struck down by haemorrhage during a routine operation?

Sometime in the night, Nicholas comes outside and wraps an arm around me. 'We'll leave in the morning.' We sit together and watch the forest and then he returns inside.

Sometime in the night, I catch you in a quick lurch downward, and wake and return you to my breast.

Sometime in the night, the dark mass of forest starts glowing and the birds announce that it is not fire, but dawn.

Inside, Nicholas is packing. I feed and change you, and we drive down the hill to the empty beach, to the deliverance of sand and water. You squint at the early morning sun and sneeze and say, 'Ahhh.' When I dip your pink foot into the icy water, it curls up like a mollusc and you start howling.

Later, when the sun is a little higher in the sky, Nicholas drives into town and returns with a new set of keys. He has found us a fibro shack with a single air-conditioning unit. We move in and pull the mattresses into the living room, and I set you up in your bouncer at my feet. As the day heats up, we lie in the cool and watch *The Sopranos*. On the screen, Ralphie beats a woman to death. I swivel your bouncer around so that you cannot see, and rock you, rock you, rock you with my foot.

RISOTTO

My childless friends are patient with tales of your exploits, or non-exploits, waiting for me to finish before gently steering the conversation to other subjects. What they fail to realise is that there are no other subjects. Sometimes, as I relate an anecdote, I recognise from my listener's look of forbearance that I have shared this story before. *It was the most extraordinary thing. He definitely said 'Hello Grandpa'!* And yet I cannot stop myself. The point is no longer entertaining an audience. The point is re-enacting your existence in words.

Perhaps you are hypnotising me; it is a type of meditation to be gazing on you, always. Your two round eyes occupy my entire field of vision, vacuuming me into your world. It is a realm of pure intuition, like music. *Me* does not yet exist there, nor *you*, only this manifold of sensation remaining to be parsed. But each day new patterns emerge. You discover which matter you have agency over – the fleshy levers of your arms, the plump swats of your hands – and which you do not. When you hear my voice, you flick your head towards me in a gesture that looks like love. But I am only another transient physical pleasure, like passing wind. I am warmth and sweetness in the mouth, the comfort of a full belly.

As you command all space, so you command all time. You shed your yesterday self without a backward glance; you inhabit a life without memory. And by living parallel to you I exist similarly. There is no longer any past tense, only present. Life contracts to the moment: comic, wonderful, desperate.

And yet your body also traps and captures time, in your burgeoning thighs, in the increasing wattage of your eyes. You are my clock, my calendar. Each morning, your face bears the imprint of a new day.

Look! Look at the baby!

You glance at the mirror and then veer back to my shoulder, until one morning you turn around for a second look.

Are we there yet?

Do you know the difference between your self and mine?

Do I?

On Facebook, I fall into intense couplings with other new mothers, virtual strangers from high school, with whom I exchange messages daily.

He's trying to roll over!

She pointed at the Cat in the Hat again, unprompted!

Another sleepless night. Could that mean he's gifted?

We tolerate each other's boasts as a tax we must pay on our

own, but we also exchange hard-won wisdom. Slowly I am assembling your owner's manual.

A late-night bottle of formula can buy you a few extra hours' sleep.

There are certain things I do not post on Facebook. The ladder of anxiety I can scale at night, if Nicholas is working late. It starts with local worries: you, in your cot, and whether you are breathing. Then it extends past the power points and appliances in the flat to the dangers that lurk outside. Hoons in cars. People who do bad things to children. Further out, to the fact of war, to the fact that mothers raise their sons and these sons are sent to die. To global warming, random meteorites, dying stars. And then finally – the endpoint of all of my reflections – to the unbearable fact of your mortality.

Is it time to retire the swaddle?

If your baby is rolling over, it's probably a good idea.

Thanks, lovely. How are you travelling?

A year ago there was no trace of your existence, and this caused me no grief. But now I cannot get beyond the wastage of it one day winking out.

I'm okay.

Only okay?

I hesitate. *A bit anxious tonight.*

Stop right there and go to bed.

It is the right advice. As I climb into bed, I take comfort from the existence of all these other mothers, logging out of Facebook to steal an hour's rest before the first feed of the night.

Each carrying their own charges – inconceivably precious, fragile as eggs teetering on spoons – as they track this dark night beside me to morning.

When you are six weeks old, Mariah offers to babysit, so that Nicholas and I can venture out to a restaurant. We discuss this for some days: it is a curiously threatening idea.

'Perhaps we could catch up on some sleep instead,' I suggest.

'Pathetic,' he says, but I can see that he is tempted.

We agree to the restaurant, finally, out of a sense of duty. To bookmark this spot; to stake out a small space of adulthood until we are again ready to occupy it. Before leaving Mariah's house, we double-check that all phones are charged, that she has memorised the latest SIDS prevention guidelines.

'You do realise I've done this before,' she grins. 'And he didn't turn out too badly, did he?'

And so we leave you and drive to a restaurant by the beach, where a waiter seats us next to the open doors and pours champagne.

'Have a happy night, folks.'

Happy. The surprise is that all this love does not quite equate to happiness. It is richer, darker than happiness. Possibly it is better than happiness. And yet. Around us, people clink their glasses and laugh. Is the rest of the world childless? Or is this what will happen one day? That I will again be able to laugh freely, without my mind listing back to you?

'How's things?' I ask Nicholas.

He takes a sip of champagne. 'Good, I suppose.'

'But?'

'I really like the baby,' he says carefully. 'But I'm not sure that I'm quite as obsessed with him as you are.'

I had noticed this. For Nicholas, you have not yet grown into your name, but are still *the baby*, a thing more than a person, a species more than an individual. A problem to be solved, through expert swaddling and best-practice burping.

'Just wait. It'll come.'

'Are you sure?'

His uncertainty touches me. 'Remember, I had a nine-month head start.'

He nods and finishes his glass. 'What about you?'

I am bored by my response, a small word, inadequate to the task.

'Tired.'

He flips open the menu, impatiently. 'Yes, I know. I'm tired too, but I think we need to stop saying it.'

He is right. It is too loaded: that one-upmanship of fatigue.

'It is the true test of a relationship, isn't it? Can I love my partner's rest as much as my own?'

He laughs. 'And the answer to that would be *no*.'

The waiter hovers. We address ourselves to the menu, but the words swim in front of me, refusing to coalesce into meaning. Perhaps this is what language is to a baby: *panko-encrusted pan-fried velouté choux beignet medallions.*

'You first,' I whisper.

'I'll have the risotto, please.'

'Make that two.'

The waiter gives us a condescending nod and withdraws. We had planned not to talk about you tonight, but not talking about you means not talking at all. And so we stare dumbly at each other, dipping bread in olive oil and blotting it in dukkah.

'Perhaps we should rethink our approach to sleep,' he offers.

My mind tracks up and down the netted sides of your porta-cot, searching for snags. Then it zooms out to the rickety staircase, and to Mariah's fat ginger cat who could mistake you for a cushion.

'That cat has been known to open doors unassisted,' I announce.

'I'm thinking of a joint sleep account,' he continues, 'into which we encourage each other to make deposits.'

As I drink more champagne, the ginger cat retreats slightly. He is still there, but his outlines are blurred.

'There's no point both of us waking up all night. If you let me sleep more, we'd have a larger sleep investment.'

I struggle to concentrate. Could this be a trick to rob me of yet more rest?

'You've obviously given this a lot of thought.'

'Just let me sleep, I'm begging you. *Let me sleep! Let me sleep!*'

I snort with laughter, inhaling some champagne, and the elderly woman at the next table turns around to watch me cough.

'Would there be compound interest on night feeds?' I ask, once I have recovered.

'Anything at all. Anything you want.'

There is something anaesthetising about this alcohol, about this sea air. It is robbing me of my defences. 'Okay, then. Let's open a sleep bank.'

'To the end of tired,' he toasts.

I laugh merrily and drink more, remembering myself. An inner springiness, a previous default state. Hope bobs up somewhere, that old familiar.

Say when! commands the waiter, brandishing an enormous pepper grinder over the risotto that is suddenly before me. I move the phone off the table into my lap, and my fine mood deflates a little. *Stay in the moment.* This surely is a lesson you are teaching me.

'So if not tired, then what?' asks Nicholas.

The risotto is luscious: leek and rice and butter merging into a single substance of comfort.

'Besotted with our child.'

Outside, a group of young people clusters around a brazier. I can smell the sea; see the twinkling fantasy of the city in the distance. We used to come down here when we first knew each other, but I cannot quite find my way back to that time. What did I used to worry about?

'And terrified. In approximately equal measure.'

'You've got to stop that, you know.'

'I know.'

It is foolish to squander your precious first months in worry. Every evening I wish you a tearful goodnight as if sending you off to war. What sort of message can that be sending?

'Remember what you said to Baba, when she was worried about Daniel? *Deal with the contractions when they come.*'

I reach for my wine glass, and the phone clatters off my lap on to the ground. As I pick it up, I surreptitiously check for messages. Nothing. But I might just text Mariah to let her know we arrived safely.

'At least wait until after we've eaten,' he says wearily.

'I'll just let her know we got here okay.'

Having a lovely time, I type, as he folds his arms and looks out to sea. *How are things on the home front?*

What is the fear, exactly? That if I relax my mind's vice-like grip, even for a moment, you will no longer be safe. That for this critical lapse into leisure we will all be punished. I wait for a text to ricochet back, but none comes.

'She's probably just dozing on the sofa,' he suggests.

'Apparently they're attracted to the milk on the baby's breath.'

'What are?'

'Cats.'

'Stop. Please. Just stop.'

Yes. And I will. Just as soon as I make this phone call.

In the car on the way home, I hold the phone aloft in order to maximise reception. 'It's probably better that we didn't have dessert,' I offer. 'More healthy.'

Nicholas stares at the road ahead. Only when the beach is far behind us does the phone vibrate in my hand.

All fine here. Take your time. Make sure you enjoy yourselves.

MOTHERS' GROUP

At home, I attempt to keep danger at bay through good housekeeping. A clean house repudiates the body's chaos, and by extension its vulnerability. My goals are modest: bread in the oven, soup on the stove, a tidy linen press stacked with clean sheets, sweet and crisp with captured sunshine. There will be fresh flowers on the table, a bowl of gleaming fruit. Somewhere the Goldberg Variations will be playing. Perhaps I will be playing them myself, as you doze under the piano, in pastel clothes with no stains on them ...

'Get a grip!' Baba says, when I share my plans. 'How is a baby going to help when you're already a *domestic cretin*?'

It is true that a baby does not help. Although you cannot yet move, you mount an olfactory as well as an aural assault on the domestic order: shit and piss and projectile vomits and even foot odour, alongside random screeches, catcalls and infant roars. And even on those rare occasions when you are silent, fatigue has its own sound – a buzz, a drone – as well as its own special effect: a hazing of the visual field, through which I can see the disorder of our flat, but cannot quite get to it.

Most days, it is easiest to abandon the problem, so I pack your nappy bag and dress you, but then you lean forward with something pressing to say, and a posset flares out like a speech bubble. As soon as I have changed you, you soil your nappy, and so we repeat the process, soaking the dirty clothes in a bucket — those endless buckets — and already it is time to feed you again, but now the dog is getting impatient and needs to be taken downstairs, and once we have returned upstairs I remember I have to express some milk for later, and now it is almost the afternoon but we will leave the flat anyway — *you can do it, girlfriend!* I coach myself, as we emerge from the door into the hallway, and a passing student backs away, alarmed — and once we have struggled down two flights of stairs I realise I have forgotten the nappy wipes, so we climb the stairs again to collect them, return to the foyer, where I buckle you in your pusher, and triumphantly burst outdoors. And here we are once again, hurtling around the oval, with you sneezing at the sun.

Some days, Fiona joins us for a walk with seven-month-old Matilda dangling from a sling around her front. Matilda is small for her age, but I am shocked by her gigantic limbs, her huge, thuggish features. Surely she is so large as to be unlovable; I cannot imagine your exquisiteness ever giving way to this.

'Pushers don't really accord with the philosophy of attachment parenting,' Fiona puffs. 'It's all about maximising skin-on-skin.'

I glance down at you sleeping in your pusher. Your hands lie folded above your rug; your nose gleams as if polished. 'What do you do at bedtime?'

'We co-sleep. The notion that infants have to be imprisoned alone in cots is completely a Western construct.' As she speaks, her baby's arms flap emphatically, underlining each of her points.

'What about naps throughout the day?'

'I nap with her.'

'But how do you ever get anything done?'

She turns to me, scandalised. 'What could possibly be more important than nurturing your child?'

I dare not mention the thank-you cards I hope to send today, let alone the beginnings of work, seeping back into my life.

'The first year of motherhood is about the baby, not the mother,' she explains. 'It's about *surrender*.'

Back at home, away from Fiona's watchful eye, I imprison you in your bassinet and address myself to the thank-you cards. It is a hopelessly ambitious undertaking, the sort of Everest of human endeavour that can only be approached one step at a time: selecting a card, identifying a recipient, remembering their gift. Once I have written in the cards – devising personalised comments about bunny rugs and teddy bears, and where possible seasoning them with small quantities of wit, or the remnants of wit, nothing too showy, actually a reassuring non-wit that only gestures at wit, in the way appropriate for a thank-you card, through the deployment of an exclamation mark, or for less discerning correspondents possibly even two: *he loves that fluffy centipede so much I'm in danger of being usurped!!* – once I have achieved all of this and taxed my creative resources to the limit, the intellectual challenge of locating the correct addresses is insurmountable, so the cards accumulate on top of the microwave, another small pocket of unmet obligation, as the noise of the flat swirls around us.

'Co-sleeping!' Baba exclaims, when I repeat this to her. 'That's what I call *creating a rod for her own back*.'

'Why?'

'What if she rolled over on her?'

'Research suggests that under certain conditions, co-sleeping might reduce the risk of cot death.'

'And where do you draw the line? Will your friend still sleep with her daughter when she's a *grown woman*?'

'You make it sound immoral.'

'It *is* immoral to set up unrealistic expectations.'

Of course it is immoral. All parenting is immoral. Hospital births are immoral, as are home births. Not breastfeeding is immoral, as is breastfeeding for too long. Asking Nicholas to give you a single bottle of formula tonight so that I can get a head start on sleep is immoral. But I surrender.

*

Late in February, Nurse Fran calls to say I have been allocated a mothers' group, meeting the following Thursday. I would like this to be a Thursday in which I leave the house with dry hair, but no sooner have I dressed you in your new overalls than you have regurgitated breakfast over us both. I commit to the full version of the pre-excursion ritual, calmly accepting that this will be a Thursday like every other.

At the Family Health Centre, the other mothers sit in an unruly circle, jiggling babies on their laps or nudging pushers by their sides.

'Good morning, ladies,' says Nurse Fran brightly. 'Welcome to your mothers' group. We'll be meeting here for the next three weeks, and then I would encourage you to keep the group going on your own.'

There is an operatic scream to our left, muted by the application of a breast. You jerk awake and stare at the baby's mohawk of hair.

'Let's begin with a brainstorming session,' continues Nurse Fran, stepping up to a blackboard. 'What's so fun about being a mother?'

There is a thoughtful silence in the room.

'Perhaps I'll get this ball rolling.' She picks up a piece of pink chalk. '*Cuddles*,' she writes, with the fat print of a primary-school teacher. 'Skin-on-skin contact is very important for mother and baby both. And let's see – what else? I know!' She changes to a pastel green chalk. '*Giggles*. Never lose your sense of humour. Who likes laughing?'

A few forlorn hands hover upwards.

'Any other suggestions?'

A pale woman with waist-length red hair clears her throat.

'The other night Thea slept straight through for three and a half hours, and I realised that sleep was the great unrequited passion of my life.'

Murmurs of assent. Nurse Fran purses her lips, but writes *sleep* on the board in mauve.

'I can go one better!' calls out the woman with the mohawked baby. '*Wine!*'

This time there is a smattering of applause.

'*Treats*,' writes Nurse Fran in lemon yellow, and then adds '*occasional*' in brackets.

'I never said anything about *occasional*!' the woman retorts, to widespread laughter.

'Well done, ladies!' Nurse Fran congratulates us. 'We're all retaining our senses of humour, which brings us back to point number two – *giggles*. But of course we don't drink alcohol while breastfeeding. I'll pass around some literature about this later on. Now comes the fun bit. I'd like you to split into groups of two and have a *conversation*. One of you will ask a question and the other one will answer it, and then you'll *swap roles*. Any questions?'

It seems you and I are in the same place: a ground zero of social interaction, from which all human behaviour must now be learnt.

'And the question I'd like you to ask is: how was your experience of childbirth?'

'How are you, love?' asks the woman beside me. 'I'm Kath, and I don't know about you, but for me labour was an absolute freakin' nightmare.' Her symmetrical features are blurred by fatigue, but in my mind I can reconstruct her pre-natal beauty.

'Why was it such a nightmare?'

'Good work,' says Nurse Fran as she patrols past. 'That's *open questioning* and *empathetic listening*.'

'The works, love. Forty-hour labour, posterior delivery, forceps. You name it, *I did it!*'

I feel a degree of performance anxiety with Nurse Fran listening. 'You poor thing. That must have been awful.'

'Very good,' Nurse Fran prompts. 'Now you might like to share a story of your own.'

I try to shape your birth into a meaningful narrative: the violation, the gross injustice of being denied an epidural. But just as I am approaching its climax, you assume a look of great pink-faced seriousness, and I remove you to the passage in search of a change-room.

When we return, the group has moved on to settling techniques. My new conversation partner, Sylvie, does not belong here. She has shiny blow-dried hair and wears a red dress that has clearly been ironed. Her baby dozes in the pram beside her, beneath a hand-knitted rug.

'I'll try *anything*,' Kath chuckles, across the room. 'Drugs for mother, drugs for baby – whatever it takes.'

'For me settling has scarcely been a challenge,' Sylvie says. 'Simply because we took an approach – how do you say? – *scientifique*. We found an excellent book, and Claude-Henri has been on the Routine from the very first day.'

'What sort of routine?'

'For example, when it is the best time for him to eat. When it is the best time for him to sleep. It is extremely well-organised.'

'What's the name of the book?' I ask urgently. But too late: Nurse Fran has heard and is looming over us.

'I must be clear: we in no way condone routines! All babies at this age have the *basic human right* to be fed on demand. This is *very disappointing*, ladies. Return to your seats, please, to watch an important video on *Keeping the Spark in Your Marriage*.'

Sylvie and Claude-Henri retreat to the other side of the room, and we sit down to watch the video, in which a man arrives home from work to an immaculate house. He presents his wife with a bouquet of flowers; she places the baby into a bassinet and turns to embrace him. You startle yourself by blowing a raspberry, but then seem pleased and do it again. I share your sentiments: this video in no way accords with our experience. Perhaps with a routine, though, things might be different; we might emerge into a world of *cuddles, giggles, sleep* and *(occasional) treats.* Perhaps Sylvie already lives there. When the video finishes, she is packed to leave. But she detours back to our side of the room, tucks a small piece of paper into my hand and then, with a toss of her glossy black hair, is gone.

Nicholas and I order the book that night and become devout converts to the Routine, synchronising our watches and setting reminder alarms throughout the day. Each morning, we wake you at 6:30, so that you can feed first from the left breast and then from the right, before I express any remaining milk in case of growth spurts. At the park with Fiona, I dare not confess that you are on a Routine, but power-walk fast enough to ensure you are back home for Morning Sleep 1B at 11:35 am. It is a train we must not miss. When you are eighty-seven days old it will become easier, as Morning Sleep 1B will be advanced to 11:45 am, allowing us an extra ten minutes' recreation time. There is a pleasing precision to these formulae: they contain all the magic of numbers, and our life takes on a new orderliness. I succeed in packing the dishwasher, in changing the sheets. We make a triumphant trip to the post office to send thank-you cards. At night, when you are crying, the Routine offers a consolation that is almost biblical. *You shall allow your child to protest for nine minutes before providing her with comfort.*

Foolishly, I mention the Routine on Facebook.

Aren't routines for control-freak working mothers?

No baby of mine is going on boot camp!

I resolve to keep the Routine a secret, and hide the copy on the refrigerator behind a magnetic calendar.

Mothers' group quickly becomes the highlight of my week. Clear personalities emerge from the debris of early motherhood – warm Kath, witty Bec, earthy Hannah – alongside hints of former lives. After we are expelled from the Family Health Centre, we meet at a café, occupying an entire table by the window. We breastfeed with a studied casualness, surreptitiously eyeing each other's technique. Outside, a group of middle-aged men drink beer around a table and leer through the window. 'You ladies are *disgusting*,' one of them splutters, as he lurches past us to the toilet.

The following week we converge on Hannah's pool, and you

bob around on your back, a floating head with frantic peddling legs. Already I am in love with every infant in the group, with the ways they reflect and amplify you: Max with his worldly, adult face; Freya with her chaotic ginger hair; Leo, six weeks younger and still unformed, until one Thursday he morphs into recognisable baby shape, grasps your hand beneath the baby gym, and together you swat the pudgy stuffed stars.

Sometimes I feel alienated, as when conversation turns to the week's baking achievements, or when Sylvie confesses that she makes her own cheese. But one Thursday, Sylvie pushes a screaming pusher in to Kath's living room and announces: 'That's it, ladies. I have had *enough*.'

Kath removes the pusher to another room, and we surround Sylvie with tea and cushions, offering a solicitude we rarely afford ourselves. 'Let it all out, darling,' we cluck, and she obliges us by crying our tears too.

SURRENDER

In a few months, Kath and Bec and Sylvie will return to full-time jobs, while I will continue my freelance existence: snatches of industry while you sleep; one-handed emails while breastfeeding; long afternoons of animal noises on the carpet. But now, as they enjoy paid maternity leave, my deadlines lurk closer and a great gulf opens between us.

Work. My secret vice.

'I just wish I were in more of a position to help you,' frets Great-Grandma Moggy over the phone.

'It's okay, Mog. I've got Nicholas.'

'Happy days! Thank *goodness* for that.'

Nicholas is so good, everyone reminds me. *He allows you to do your work.* And he is. Of all the fathers I know, he is the most involved in his child's care. But I cannot help register the double standard. 'When Nicholas works, he's a breadwinner,' I complain to Baba. 'But when I work, it's self-indulgence.'

'You just can't win,' she agrees. 'When you were born, I never heard the end of it: *what about your medical degree?* And then I went back to study, and it was *what about that dear little baby?* But you've got to give Nicholas some credit, too. He *is* good.'

On Monday mornings, I surrender you to him and jog down the road to the conservatorium. 'Where is *him?*' demands the college housekeeper, as I hurtle back at lunch-time, enraged by slow pedestrians, desperate to hear of your latest breakthrough. When I burst into the flat, I find you guffawing wildly at Nicholas's pig impersonation. Why do you never find me funny?

'It's happened,' he tells me, and I can see it in his face as he looks at you. 'I've fallen in love.' The following week, under his watch, you discover the letter W, a particular wobble of the chin while vocalising – *wa wa wa wa*. Secretly I wish you had saved it for me.

Soon it will be time to return to the concert stage. I imagine I still know how to play: I can feel the imprints of the keys on my fingers, the precise angles of sound. But when I sit down at the piano, I am shocked by my clumsiness. I devote your nap time to rehabilitative practice; when you awake, I arrange you in your high chair at the treble end of the piano, where you bang out a gleeful descant.

'There's no prize for being the multi-tasking genius of the world,' Nicholas tells me, but there is. The prize is more time with you. Sometimes a colleague suggests coffee, and I stare back at him in disbelief. Why would I squander our time apart on *coffee?*

Housekeeping is a vanity I can no longer afford. When Mariah comes over to visit, she wordlessly addresses herself to the unmade beds, to the stalled laundry, to the festering kitchen. Probably I should feel shame at this, but all I feel is relief.

In March, I fly to Sydney for advance promotion of my first book, a musical memoir which I have not yet completed. It is a Thursday, so I will miss mothers' group, akin to skipping a critical episode of a favourite television series: what if Leo has started to laugh? If Freya has rolled over? But I express as much milk as possible, don the clothes of a previous life and leave you at home with Mariah.

She peers at the Routine, dubiously. 'I wouldn't want to wake a sleeping baby.'

But she must, or the whole system will collapse! 'Yesterday we were five minutes late for the 11:10 wake-up,' I caution her. 'We spent the whole afternoon playing catch-up.'

The taxi beeps for a second time.

'Enjoy yourself, darling, and don't give us a second's thought. We'll have a great time, this wee man and myself.'

At the airport, I see babies everywhere. Each of their cries triggers a small letdown, a gentle interior needling, as if my breasts had the ambition to feed all the children of the world. And then I am on an aeroplane, travelling away from you at eight hundred kilometres an hour, next to a businessman in a striped pink shirt. His arm presses importantly against mine, moist and spicy with deodorant. Then it slackens and he starts to snore, leaving me alone in the company of this other stranger: myself.

What is it that adults do when alone? I glance through a book, but the words do not stick, so I channel-surf through the audio programmes, seeking a station that speaks to my condition – the amputation that is your absence, the way I crave you with my flesh. *I want your body, baby, I want it now …* sings a woman, but it is wrong, all wrong, speaking of sexual desire. I cannot remember how that ever seemed a good idea. When we hit turbulence, I remain calm. The excursion feels almost frivolous for its absence of risk: if the plane crashes, you will not be killed.

As soon as we land, I phone Mariah. The businessman jerks awake and points sternly at the lambent seatbelt sign.

'How is he?' I whisper.

'Good as gold. Nothing to worry about.'

There is a suspicious, muffled exclamation close to the phone, even though it is officially time for Morning Nap 2A, but now the hostess is approaching and I quickly hang up. When the seatbelt light is snuffed out I call back, but the phone is engaged. I try again from the taxi and there is no response. Perhaps I should call Nicholas and ask him to go home and check? No. *Deal with the contractions when they come*. Instead, I take out my notes to distract myself. At the conference, I will be playing the piano and talking about my memoir – talking about me! – but already I am bored by myself, so I close my eyes and think of you instead. Your toes like baby grapes. The yeasty smell of your scalp.

As soon as I arrive at the venue, I search for a bathroom in which I can express. Afterwards, clutching the warm jar of my milk, I emerge into an enormous warehouse crowded with stalls, with posters of books and authors, with the great hubbub of the literary enterprise.

'There you are!' calls out a publicist. 'Would you like to store that ... beverage?' I follow her to a kitchen, feeling vaguely reprimanded by the trapezium of honey-blonde hair. 'Now there's something you should know: the organisers have moved your performance to the foyer, because they couldn't shift the piano. But I think this is even better. There'll be a captive audience.'

Back in the foyer, I glimpse the piano, before the doors of the auditorium are thrown open and an excited crowd swarms out, encircling the instrument until it disappears. I see vaguely familiar faces – a celebrated poet, a well-known publisher – faces that carry a faint, archaeological lustre from a previous life. They descend avidly upon the morning tea.

An organiser guides me through the crowd to the small island of the piano and hands me a microphone. 'Just start when you're ready. Everybody will stop and listen.'

'*I definitely saw Tsiolkas,*' a woman exclaims. '*I'd recognise him anywhere.*'

There is a single, empty row of chairs next to the piano, and I turn towards it now and clear my throat.

'When my publisher asked me to write a memoir, my immediate thought was *moi*? A memoir?'

The crowd noise continues around us, echoing this sentiment, as the publicist takes a seat in front of me, offering an encouraging smile.

'Who did I think I was, writing a memoir?'

A man in a navy parka sits down at the far left, cradling a lamington like a small pet.

'If I hadn't met my teacher, I certainly wouldn't have become a pianist.'

I am not entirely sure what I am talking about. Am I in fact still a pianist? Or am I just the envoy of a deceased self? My old clothes hang strangely on my body, a fact which is in itself suspicious.

'Writing this book offered me a chance to clarify my own thinking about music …'

Back home, my mothers' group would be meeting about now, talking about nappy services or settling techniques. Freya might have started cooing; Max might have perfected his clap. There are great things going on out there, but here I am hundreds of kilometres away from you, talking to a row of chairs about *myself*, an entity I no longer much believe in. *What could possibly be more important than nurturing your child?* The man in the parka takes a delicate bite of his lamington, then blissfully closes his eyes. A woman sits beside him, and frowns at me through oversized glasses, as if identifying a beetle. There are now three people in my audience, at least two of whom are awake.

'Perhaps I will read you an excerpt,' I offer.

Around us, the crowd surges with enthusiasm for books other than mine.

'*Oh yes, of course. I know the vet who inspired Aisha …*'

'*Heard John Banville speak in the tents …*'

Who would have thought that book lovers could be so noisy? That they would bang their crockery with so much vigour?

'*More of a friend of a friend …*'

'*Of course the sorts of books that women read are not …*'

I take out my manuscript. 'It was my grandfather who found her.'

'*Gave Fred the Undercover Kitty her vaccinations …*'

'I was nine years old,' I continue. 'And had been learning piano from a local jazz teacher …'

My breasts are filling again with milk, pressing against my shirt, reminding me that my place is not here.

'It sat well with the grand narrative I had in mind for my life,' I say, as a stripy haystack veers in from the left. I register its bulbous, doleful nose just moments before it collides into my side, bouncing off like a dodgem car.

'Sorry,' it whispers, huskily.

The man in the parka sits upright. 'It's GRUG! Grug's here, folks!'

My two other audience members swivel their attention to the haystack, glance back at me, and then follow the haystack's jolly progression through the crowd, as it dispenses autographs. I feel a new pressure in my tear ducts, from humiliation or mirth or perhaps both, as though my body seeks to expose me, exploding back into liquid components before this row of chairs.

'Perhaps the best thing now would be to play for you,' I suggest, putting the manuscript down. It is the first time I have performed since you were born, and I am not sure if I still know how to do it, but I need to remember, both to silence this audience and to quell my tears. I wait for a moment of quiet, and when none is forthcoming I place my hands on the keyboard like a prayer. But amidst the din of morning tea, in this giant auditorium, my playing is mute, silent. I can see my hands moving on the keys, but I can no longer remember what the result sounds like.

Back at home that afternoon, after Mariah has left, you wake crying and I carry you into bed with me to feed. *I surrender*, I call out to the Routine pasted to the fridge; to the book that needs to be completed; to the computer with its plaintive Facebook postings: *Did you get my message about Isla's first push-up?* Outside the flat, the college hums with life, but here inside is my solipsistic, subversive bliss, lying in bed with you, occupying both of our bodies at once. The sweetness of relief in emptying the breast, its gradual deflation, fine and exquisite as pissing; and at the same time – a part of the transaction I feel even more keenly – the sweetness of the milk entering your mouth. You unspool it from the breast, organise it rhythmically in your throat, and send it swirling down to your stomach – gulp-swallow-pause, gulp-gulp-gulp – so that you seem to grow larger beneath my hand. For a while my mind tracks idly between you and me, but then it remains somewhere in between, as when drifting to sleep with one's hands interlaced, unable to unravel the sensation of finger on hand or hand on finger. Gradually your sucking becomes less rhythmic, and the suction of your mouth loosens until you release my nipple into the air with a small pop, cool with your saliva, and now we are both asleep.

LIFE

SLEEP

One morning I wake up and discover that my newborn has gone. I fold up your first round of baby clothes to give away – tiny flannel bodysuits, kimonos the size of handkerchiefs – and realise from the lump in my throat that I love even these small scraps of cloth, for containing the residue of your evaporated self. Nobody warned me that a newborn would be so transient. I wasted our precious months together waiting to see who you would become, waiting for you to open your eyes, to smile, to laugh. And now, like a dream, that newborn has vanished entirely from my memory, leaving only these clothes with their faint milky smell.

The compensation is that this new you is even more wonderful, a technology that forever upgrades itself. Up close you have a bestial wildness, commanding my body with a lover's entitlement. You grab my spectacles and tweak my nipples, and seize the inside of my mouth with your fingers. Your feet accumulate fluff, even though they take you nowhere; your head absorbs smells. Each evening at bath-time I sink my nose into your hair for an olfactory history of your day: the perfumed babysitters, the wine-drinkers and onion-eaters, Nicholas's sweetness, the chess smell of Pop. If I burrow my nose in deeper, I can escape the adult world entirely.

Every day you acquire more purchase over the world, so that there are places now where I can meet you in wonder. At night in your nursery, I switch on the magic lantern and track the blurry lamb's passage across the ceiling, absorbing the great weight of your silence in my lap. When you wake in the morning, we count the animals in your farmyard book, your miniature forefinger in my hand like a pencil, guiding me, teaching me how to look.

One morning I teach you how to roll over, but the following day you have already forgotten. You lie on your stomach, fisted arm straining above your head, arched torso insistent. When it is time for your first food, the sight of rice porridge on a spoon outrages you – the presumption of it! But then I slip it between your lips and you are astonished into silence. You savour this new sensory experience – the grainy texture in the mouth, the gustatory explosion in the brain – nod like a wine connoisseur and open your mouth for more. Systematically we move through the major fruit and vegetable purees. You discover an intimate joy in eating, in shovelling apple into your mouth, rubbing it into your eyes and hair, but it is also a lesson in loss. Unlike the breast milk that you were born to, food is a zero-sum thing. When you love it so much you eat it quickly, and then it is gone.

One night, our sleep is interrupted by the alarm of your baby monitor. Our bodies teleport us to the sides of your cot, where you have rolled off your movement sensor, and are snuffling gently in your sleep, ignoring the siren that announces your death. It is a complicated pleasure, parenthood. I had imagined it might be about reliving childhood, but it is more often about being on lookout: awake, responsible, grown-up.

Despite our adherence to the Routine, you begin waking every morning at 3:14, regular as an appointment. There is no mention of this in the book, and I begin to lose faith in its doctrines. I no longer try to settle you in your cot, but smuggle you into bed beside me. For a few moments you remain silent, the chubby crescent of your body curled into mine, the soft nape of your neck beneath my fingers. But then you turtle up your head and start crawling. All night you squirm and wriggle, like my own insomniac mind. You reject the law of parallel sleeping, wedging yourself sideways so that we are pushed to the far edges of the mattress.

'This isn't working for me,' Nicholas growls from beneath his pillow.

You lodge your solid head into the crook of my neck, beating down on my torso with jackhammer legs; you stretch out and float like a star. When I start to drift off, you pull yourself up on the bedhead and collapse into free-fall; I jerk awake just in time to catch the giant coconut of your head. Towards daybreak you bunch your nappy into my face and fall asleep, and I doze to the smell of urine.

'I don't understand what happened,' laments Nicholas. 'The Routine was working so well.'

One night, as I roam sleeplessly through the flat, I hear an alarm in your room. It beeps until you awake and then stealthily falls silent. In the morning Nicholas pulls the bags down from the top of your closet and discovers the culprit – an ancient travel clock – stashed in the bottom of a backpack. He removes it from the room and confiscates its batteries. But the damage has been done. The 3:14 wake-up has become part of your routine, written into the rhythms of your body, your diurnal cycle.

Over the weeks that follow, your sleep regresses further, until you are waking twice a night, and soon three times. I am too depleted to fight and keep you in bed with me, where you wake every hour, returning to sleep only if you are feeding in total darkness, with my hair coiled around your forefinger. Sleep becomes an ideal, a sort of perfected human state. I daydream about it while doing the dishes; at the piano I seek its particular sweetness in my sound. A friend recommends sleep school, but there is no time, and at any rate taking this sort of large decision is no longer possible. In August, Baba accompanies us to Sydney to mind you while I rehearse. For a week she shares your afternoon nap without protest; each night, she observes us co-sleeping without comment. Only at the airport does she stage an intervention: 'This cannot go on. He's got to go cold turkey.'

At home, I try cold turkey for half an hour. There is a daytime logic in getting you to sleep in your cot, but the night has rules of its own. When you wake crying, my body has to bring you into bed with me. You will be happier there and so will I, and tomorrow's tiredness will look after itself.

*

In October, we surrender and enrol in sleep school. The introductory session takes place in a giant playroom with alphabet friezes on the walls and wooden blocks on the floor.

Other parents crouch on small plastic chairs pushed up against the walls: a web designer whose baby will only doze while feeding; a rural beautician and her plumber husband, whose baby sleeps for a maximum of thirty minutes a night. An elegant Somali woman sits on the floor, with her glossy twin boys lying beside her. You are attracted to the confectionary pink of their palms and crawl over for an experimental taste, before scrambling back into the middle, panting like a dog.

'He's certainly energetic,' remarks the Mothercraft nurse.

'I'd just come to the end of my tether,' says a welder, his arm slung around a faded wife. 'The missus was going crazy. The only way I could get the kids to sleep was by driving. Don't get me wrong, I love my car. For the blokes here, it's a WRX. You know, a Suby.'

Beside me, Nicholas attempts an appreciative noise.

'How long did you need to drive before they fell asleep?' the nurse asks.

'Two hours, on a good night. But if I opened the door, they'd wake up. So I slept in the Suby too.'

'And would they stay asleep all night?'

'Until about 3, then I'd drive for another couple of hours. It'd bring us home, at least.'

'How long have you been doing this for?'

'Since Aiden was a baby, I guess. What's that – three years?'

There are sympathetic clucks around the room, but Nicholas and I exchange looks. We had not considered driving you to sleep: it might yet be the solution.

Later that evening, we discover that sleep school offers different solutions. Scattered down the corridor are the other mothers. In this state, it is hard to tell them apart – teary, misshapen, wearing pyjamas – but each of their babies has a distinctive ringtone. Next door, a baby girl bleats furiously; down the corridor, a little boy performs a percussive *haka*. I wish they would protest more loudly, so that I could not hear your cry. Your husky lament, based on a minor second. A pause, and then ascent to scream. Surely it has been two minutes already?

The nurse makes her leisurely way back down the passage. 'You can go in and comfort him now, dear.'

But the only way I can comfort you is to bring you into bed with me, lie you on your right side and feed you with my hair coiled around your forefinger, and this is no longer allowed.

When I open the door to your room, you are jumping up and down in your cot, your mouth turned down at the sides like a ferocious carp. I lie you down and pat your stomach, as the nurse instructs, but you arch your back and smack my hand away.

'I don't think he wants you to comfort him, dear,' she offers, so I turn my back on your cry and follow her back into the corridor. It is a new way of measuring time: four minutes equals thirteen screams, eight hiccups, three aggrieved shouts. Now a torrent of invective, directed against neglectful parents: *wub wub wub wub wub wub wub!*

'Oh, isn't he *angry*,' she marvels. 'He's furious with you!'

I hold on to this thought. Outrage I can cope with: outrage, surely, is empowering. But after four minutes, when I am allowed back in, I press my hand against your chest and feel your tiny heart palpitating. She lied. You are scared.

'Give him his comforter,' she whispers.

I pass you the cloth rabbit I have selected to be your mother substitute, and you snatch it from my hand and fling it out of the cot. Why are we doing this again? I think of Fiona, snugly asleep in bed with Matilda. *The notion that infants have to be imprisoned alone in cots is completely a Western construct.* 'We're training them in individualism,' I had explained to my book club, before we came.

'How sad,' said Dave, who lives by himself. 'We're training them in loneliness.'

Surely a baby cannot scream forever. Surely a baby has to sleep at some time. This must be an immutable law of nature. But now your scream is the scream of the child abandoned on Mount Taygetos, of the orphan of war, of the newborn left in a dumpster. It is the scream of a child who knows that aloneness is dangerous, that away from his mother, death is closer.

'Are you okay, dear?' asks the nurse. She is infinitely patient, infinitely compassionate, and I realise I despise her.

Over the course of the night, other babies surrender to sleep, but your screams grow louder. Sometimes they wind down for a moment – the briefest pause – and then return with renewed grievance, as though the situation has been examined from another perspective and adjudged even worse. The witching hour comes and goes; the second hand continues its dumb slow progress, round and round and round. Two minutes. Four minutes. Six minutes. I remember those first screams ten months ago, the violence of that first cleaving. And I start thinking of a later violence too. *Your cot is lonely as the grave.* The second hand grows fat behind my tears. *I am forcing you to confront your own mortality.*

At 5 am, in desperation, I take you into the bedroom to give you to Nicholas. There seems to be someone in bed with him, but that is beside the point: 'He's all yours.'

He sits up with uncharacteristic alacrity. Then he turns into the beautician. 'You're in the wrong room, sweetie.'

Her baby girl jerks awake from her thirty minutes of nightly slumber, and I slink out of the room.

The following morning, the kitchen is commandeered by the other mothers, all of whom know instinctively where to find the tea towels.

'How did you go last night?'

'Things were looking better for a moment,' murmurs the beautician, 'but there was an interruption.'

You sit in your high chair, surveying the room, betraying no evidence of last night's activities other than a neat black bag under each of your eyes. When I bring you breakfast, you reward me with a radiant smile.

'Aren't you a good boy?' says the new Mothercraft nurse. 'You can have a small play before your morning catnap.'

I know a morning catnap will never happen, but after playtime I take you back into your bedroom. 'It's time for your catnap,' I explain, crouching beside you; you reach through the bars and anchor your fingers firmly to my nose. When I attempt nasal withdrawal, you make a preliminary protest, a small opening sally, and I realise I do not have the strength to follow this through. So, while the nurse checks on the baby girl down the corridor, I seize you from your cot, run into my bedroom and shut the door.

'Shhh!' I warn you, as you offer a complicit smile.

Nicholas has left for a meeting, so I phone Sash in Adelaide and rehearse my excuses. 'He slept in this morning, and I knew that he would never go down this afternoon if I insisted on a catnap.'

There is a stern silence. 'You're the problem here, you know that? You're his *enabler*.'

The nurse's sensible footsteps pause outside the door.

'There's no point being there if you're going to be disobedient. Now go and find the nurse and confess.'

Fatally, you choose this moment to begin your happy song – 'a-*dya*, a-*dya*.' For the rest of the day, the nurse does not leave our side.

We were told not to bring work to sleep school, but I have previously agreed to interview a pianist in China for a profile article. That evening, it is Nicholas's turn to settle you, so I apply the ear plugs and attempt to sleep. When I remove them at midnight, both you and Nicholas are silent. I creep out to the front desk, and ask the night nurse if I can borrow a speaker phone, in order to record the interview.

'We don't really encourage parents to bring work into sleep school,' she explains, but unplugs the phone anyway. I switch on the pale night lights in the playroom, and the toy dinosaurs and tricycles cast large shadows on the walls. There is an initial screech from the speaker, and then the pianist's voice booming through the room.

'Yes, I was child of Cultural Revolution.'

I move through my questions and take notes, congratulating myself on my midnight multi-tasking, on my ability to get work done even while teaching you how to sleep. Somewhere a baby is crying, but my body does not protest so it must not be you.

'There is something I feel that is very close to Chinese culture: Bach is always looking for peace.'

A teenage mother sits wide-eyed at the kitchen table, drinking coffee. From down the passage I hear a gentle Somali lullaby.

'After all the crazy life, the crazy time, we are really looking for that peace. Do you understand?'

'Yes, I understand.'

After we finish the interview, I return the phone to the nurse.

'Everything go okay, dear?'

I nod, and she plugs the phone back in without saying anything. But she does not need to. I know that I am the problem.

*

The following afternoon, Nicholas and I are guided into a small classroom for a group session on Team Parenting, while you and the other children remain in the playroom. It is one of the few times we have been together without you since your birth, and as we sit down at a laminated desk, it has some of the novelty of a first date.

'Let's start with a brainstorming session,' a social worker suggests. 'What is a family?'

Never have I brainstormed more fervently than since becoming a mother; never have I felt less sure of what I know.

'This is a more complicated question than you realise,' she continues. 'For instance, what do we call all those single people in the community?'

'Losers!' offers the welder.

His wife cuffs him, laughing; the social worker's face hardens. 'What I am seeking is a more inclusive definition. What defines a family?'

'A family loves and cares for each other,' the web designer suggests.

Someone gave you a book along these lines, which I retired from your bookshelf shortly afterwards. *Families like to hold hands and cuddle. Families come in lots of different shapes and sizes and colours, but all families are made from a magical substance called love.*

'It's definitely about love,' the welder concedes.

The social worker writes the word *love* up on the board, and we sit there staring at it. From down the corridor I can hear your happy noise: 'a-*dya*, a-*dya*.'

'I wasn't expected to be so blind-sided by love,' the web designer continues. 'They should come with a warning sign that says *danger*.'

There is pained laughter from around the room, a new air of confession, of communal vulnerability.

The plumber clears his throat. 'It's a great thing being a dad.' Then he blushes and drops his voice. 'I reckon it's about the best thing a bloke can do.'

After dinner, it is time for you and me to resume our duel, and I brace for another torturous night. Who would have thought that teaching a baby to sleep should be one of the great life challenges? But this time, after six minutes, when I go in and pat you, you become quiet and turn to me with giant forgiving eyes. The nurse gestures that it is time to leave, but I pretend not to see and remain on the floor beside you. You tap a gentle percussion on my fingernail and then fall asleep, clinging to my thumb.

The nurse is still waiting by the door, and I attempt to extract my thumb from your grasp. It is a delicate late-night Tai Chi, stillness in motion. Afterwards I leave my hand suspended above your body for several moments, so you can feel its halo of warmth, and then I withdraw that too. In the most precarious part of the whole operation, I move back to my haunches and stand to exit the darkened room. My knee cracks loudly; opening the door floods the room in half-light; but you continue to sleep.

'You're making progress,' the nurse tells me. 'But next time you need to leave the room earlier. It's for your own wellbeing.'

Of course she is right. Now that you are asleep, it all makes sense to me. But four hours later I wake in panic at your silence.

'It's called sleep,' Nicholas murmurs. 'It's what normal people do. *Don't go in.*'

I lie awake for another twenty minutes, wishing you would say something, until I am relieved to hear your cry. But this time, as I bound into your room, your protest has less intensity, or am I imagining it? There is an experimental cough, a hiccup that sounds recreational.

'Lie down, darling,' I whisper, patting the mattress. 'Lie down.'

You plop down on your nappy, startled. Then you lower yourself on to your side. I rest a hand on your stomach and wait with you in the darkness. From the way your stomach feels under my palm, I can tell that your eyes are open, and that now they are closed.

At the end of the week, we embrace the nurses gratefully and exchange email addresses with the other parents. There is talk of a Christmas barbecue; of course we will stay in touch.

After we have returned home, there are a few group emails, and then they taper off. But you continue sleeping through the night. At 11 pm you stir, shouting once before returning to sleep. All three of us are better rested, and I remember what it is to be an adult, to have a short-term memory, a measure of tolerance. And yet I feel bereft. I miss you for the eleven hours we are apart at night. I want you back in bed with me, with my palm over the drum of your tummy and my fingertips against your chest, feeling your small, busy heart tapping out its code, its *dum-dum-dum*, the only message I need to hear.

OUTINGS

In November you invent walking, taking two small steps before plonking back down on your nappy, unconvinced. But the following week you try again, mastering four steps and then five, until you are stumbling across the lounge room – each step a stopped fall – laughing like a thrill-seeker. What provokes such a rash act? Is it merely imitation, or some deeper genetic imperative? In the twenty months since your conception you have traced the evolution of man: from amoeba to amphibian to quadruped, and now this cackling biped.

Walking is a greater thrill when accessorised with a held object, with blusher brush or electric toothbrush. Your newly liberated hands are two small mouths, hungry for sustenance, for mischief. You take a fork from the cutlery drawer and introduce it to the power point; you push a chair against the side of the balcony and climb up, ready to launch yourself into air. We move the adult world a little higher, but nothing is safe. Even the carpet is malevolent, rising daily to hit you, so that your face accumulates bruises and grazes and black eyes, a child battered by the planet.

After a week of walking, you have developed a swagger, a new ownership of the world. 'He is quite a statesmanlike one-year-old,' remarks the college's Chinese tutor. Every morning I release you into the corridor, where you approach the vacuum cleaner with a particular gait – left leg stretched in front of you, gulping distance – and press the *on* button. If it is not plugged in, you supply the noise: *waaah!* Sometimes, while guarding the stairwell, I join you in your noise-making, trying to appreciate the small things in life, the thrill of suction, but I struggle to achieve your level of mindfulness. An orange balloon bobs down the passage; when the dog bites it, it turns loudly to rubber. You jerk towards me, and I explain about popping, about the transient nature of balloons, but you shake your head and charge into a student's room.

'Hello, gorgeous!' she says, pleased at the distraction.

Encouraged, you try another room, and then another, until you stride out with the resurrected orange balloon.

'It's not actually the same one,' I falter, but in your triumphant laugh my world view is already discredited.

I purchase a seat for you at the front of my bike, and we spend fugitive days together on the road, spotting diggers, sharing a rapture of the mechanical world. You have taught me a new way of looking: '*Fwut!*' you declare, upon spotting a truck, so that even when alone I feel a small flare of delight upon seeing one. At the playground, you approach a small girl at the slippery dip, press her surprised nose like a button and retreat to the seesaw. A group of teenage boys pauses at soccer so you can swing at the ball with your foot; after you make contact, you strut through a family picnic, offering the grandmother a high five.

At the pool, I instruct you in water. 'This is *water*. We are about to get *wet*!'

A veteran mother lounges beside us, with close-cropped hair and a ravaged bohemian face.

'Water is *wet*, not dry!' I proclaim.

She shoots me a look of such contempt that I feel ashamed by the voice – over-enunciated, all-knowing – still ringing in my ears. It is as invasive as a stranger shouting into a phone on a tram, and as one-sided, a voice I recognise from my childhood as Baba's *voice of instruction*. How readily I have embraced this version of motherhood. Perhaps I name things less for your benefit than for my own, for the great pleasure of show and tell, of offering this world up to you. But there is also comfort to be had from such factual pronouncements. While conversing with a group of colleagues I notice a helicopter flying overhead, and wait for an appropriate pause in which to point it out.

At the zoo, I offer you the gift of creatures, introducing you to the animals that populate your books. But the creatures are less interesting than your face as you register them: your clear uncomplicated brow, your round hungry eyes.

'That's a giraffe. See his long neck?'

You find it fascinating, but no more fascinating than the boy beside us with the whistle, or his mother with the tattoo on her breast.

'That's a giraffe,' she announces from the same script. 'See his long neck?'

We investigate the disappointed apes, the sulky great cats, the platypus swimming in autistic circles. 'Dah!' you point, as an orang-utan hangs casually on a branch. He plunges downwards and then catches himself with a long elastic arm, and you sob violently, as if slapped. In the marmoset enclosure, a monkey with a baby on her back approaches the viewing window, urinates on her hand and drinks it. I register no surprise on your face; everything is equally strange and wonderful. The baby climbs off her back and moves past the ogling adults and flashing cameras until he finds your face. He presses his nose against the window and you lean into him, matching his wide eyes and outstretched arms, consciousness self-regarding.

At the children's farm, you sit alongside the other children on the tractor, disguised as just another child, like a superhero in civilian clothes. Only I am aware of your distinction, spectating on your life with my idiot grin. Around us, parents broadcast the names of their children – *'Isabella!' 'Jackson!'* – small declarations of class, of aspiration. Their voices are coercive and impatient, unwilling to experience this child's excursion at a child's tempo. *'Come and see the pigs!'*

You are enchanted by the hen, but she is straggly and unprepossessing, and surely not the best investment of our farm time.

'*Come and see the pigs!*' As I lift you on to the fence of the pig pen, a giant black sow emerges from the enclosure, with hairy moist snout and contemptuous eyes. She approaches with a loud bristling snort, and you launch yourself off the fence into my arms, weeping. It is your first monster sighting, and even a return visit to the tractor cannot console you.

That night you have your first attack of the night terrors. When I go into your room, I find you hyperventilating, drenched with sweat, your eyes open but unseeing. I rock you, singing through all your nursery rhymes, trying to remake your baby world in shades of cream and pink, but you cannot be roused or consoled. 'It's the pig,' I explain to Nicholas, when he comes in to check. It is some time before your sobs subside and the giant sow returns to her enclosure, at least for now.

*

It seems important for you to have music in your life, so sometimes I set you up in your high chair for my trio rehearsals. You stare solemnly at the sounds being drawn out of the instruments, and then shout for Nicholas to come to your rescue. I bring you to a concert I am reviewing, of a toy piano specialist, and you listen in rapt silence, letting out an exuberant hooray only during the applause. The pianist pauses in her bowing and squints out to the audience: 'In case your baby gets restless, can you please take him out, because it makes it difficult for me?'

I am so enraged I mention it in my review. How could she

imagine that a silent auditorium was more important than your education? Does she not know *who you are*? But the following week I am in Adelaide, performing with my trio. Two former schoolmates, with whom I enjoyed a brief but passionate affair on Facebook, sit in the dress circle with their babies. As we play, the babies gurgle and shout and cry, defacing the canvas of the auditorium's silence, vandalising our sound. My colleagues shoot me panicked looks. *But it is not him!* I want to announce to the hall. *My baby is at home with his grandmother!* We struggle to concentrate, and feel the audience struggling with us.

Afterwards, the stage manager approaches us. 'There were a number of complaints about the noise. Were they your friends?'

'Not really,' I say, as one of the mothers appears backstage with her pusher. 'This is Isla,' she smiles, as though Isla were a celebrity I had always yearned to meet. Isla stares back at me, pink-eyed and unrepentant. She is a very plain baby, really.

There is a clear hierarchy of babies, I realise. Although I love all babies in the abstract, there is really only one baby. Then there is the inner circle – the shared young of family and friends and mothers' group – and finally there are all the other babies of the world. Civilisation lies in pretending otherwise. In defending other babies against you in the playground; in insisting you return the bucket and spade even when *their mothers are not looking*. One morning you chance upon the small gallery of our friends' babies, stuck to the refrigerator, and rip off the bottom row, howling in dismay. When we introduce you to your new cousin Olive, you smile politely and attempt to remove her eye.

At the museum, as I explain metamorphosis to you, a baby crawls past the caterpillar display. A look of pure malice washes over your features – a look you have not yet learnt to conceal – and you run after her, attacking with a pinch. The baby freezes for a moment, processing this sudden change in circumstance, and then starts wailing.

'Don't worry, sweetheart,' says her mother, swooping down to pick her up. 'The big boy is just trying to say hello.'

Mortified, I redirect you towards the wombat. *There is always one pincher at playgroup*, Fiona has told me, *and the greatest shame is when that pincher is your child.* Your next target is a baby boy, gurgling at the turtle. Before I have had time to intercept, you have pinched and run, chortling loudly.

'I didn't even realise you knew how to pinch,' I announce to the room. '*We do not pinch at home!*'

The baby's mother picks him up, offering me a complicit smile: 'The little boy's just learning how to be gentle.'

I move you towards the spiders, but you are quick and devious, crawling through tunnels too small for me, feigning interest in Duplo and then attacking. Behind my shame, I am also a little amused. Hunting babies demonstrates a certain chutzpah, a certain character. It is certainly a lot funnier than somebody else's baby hunting you. But when you reoffend near the colouring-in station, the other mothers no longer make eye contact, and it is time for us to go home.

*

'He's certainly a very *active* baby,' observes Fiona. 'Do you think you might be over-stimulating him?'

'Nonsense,' says Nicholas. 'He just needs to be socialised. It's like puppy training.'

And so we begin your socialisation with Reading Time at the local library. As usual, we are running late and the dishwasher is dirty, so I decide not to bring your water bottle. Instead, I throw an opened packet of sultanas into my bag and – in a moment of inspiration – grab Sylvie's Tupperware container from on top of the microwave. It is a Tupperware container purchased especially for the storage of baby rice cakes, which she had produced when I forgot to bring your snack to mothers' group: 'I always pack a spare.' We had all admired its compact dimensions, the gratifying way its circumference encompassed the small circle of rice cake.

Outside the library, I remove you from your seat, chain up the bicycle, and tip the sultanas out of my bag into the Tupperware container. As we run in, I brandish it like an entry card, so that the other mothers can recognise me as one of their own kind. They are arranged in an orderly circle in the Reading Room, with their compliant charges on their laps. In the middle, a fleshy story-teller sits poised upon a milkmaid's stool.

'Good morning, everyone,' she says. 'Let's start with the *Hello* song.'

I do not know the words of the *Hello* song but attempt to lip-synch, as you propel yourself off my lap to range through the room, investigating the water bottles of other children.

'Hello hello hello, How are you?'

As you approach the water bottles, the other mothers neatly confiscate them, removing them from your reach while continuing to sing. I notice for the first time that you have a runny nose, but I have forgotten to bring tissues.

'Hello hello hello, Let's clap our hands! Good idea!'

Near the bookcase, a small girl drinks from her pink bottle, places it carefully back on the carpet and then clambers into her mother's lap. You crawl towards the bottle purposefully. It is important that I intercept before it makes contact with your runny nose, but you are too quick, ducking under a chair to grab it. Then you turn to address the audience, holding the water bottle aloft, your unwiped nose plain for all to see.

'That's mine!' wails the little girl. Her mother casts me an admonishing look, the first acknowledgement of our existence since arrival. In desperation, I rattle the Tupperware container and open its lid, flashing the sultanas at you flagrantly. You hesitate for a moment, release the water bottle and run towards me.

'Hello hello hello. I'm good! I'm great! I'm wonderful!'

The mother quarantines the water bottle in a plastic sandwich bag and files it away in her nappy bag.

'But Mummy, it's mine!' whispers her child.

'You can't have it now, Aurelia. It's *dirty*.'

I attempt to wipe your nose with a wet nappy wipe – an unsatisfying, smearing experience – as you grab the Tupperware, tipping the sultanas into an unruly pyramid on the carpet. I notice that they have acquired detritus from my handbag: a pink paper clip, an unidentifiable foreign coin, the fluffy dandruff of ancient tissue. From somewhere, I hear a *tsk*.

When the *Hello* song finishes, the story-teller fetches some picture books, and the mothers around me coalesce into small groups. From their rapport, their ease with each other's children, I realise I am in the presence of other mothers' groups.

'I haven't seen Charlotte wear that t-shirt before.'

'Oh, bless!'

'I found a fantastic shop online.'

I know these lines – I rehearse them every week with my own group – and attempt to join in. 'How did anyone ever raise children before online shopping?'

There is a pause before the conversation resumes.

'Is Richard still enjoying his new position?'

I am stung, restored to high school in one quick moment. The injustice of it! This might not be my mothers' group, but it easily could have been. What is it that disqualifies me? Your runny nose? My failure to pack your water bottle? Or is it the overly eager way I try for eye contact? There is something tribal about this, the deeply embedded loyalty of ancient bloodlines. You will not be admitted and neither will I. I turn my attention to our nappy bag, instead, and notice for the first time its patina of sediment, the ubiquitous browning of our shared life.

'Shall we do some Incy Wincy?' asks the story-teller.

'Yes, please!' gush the mothers, more loudly than the children. 'Hooray!'

'Spider!' I call to the back of the room, where you are preparing to launch yourself from a bookshelf. '*Your favourite thing!*'

Another group singalong begins, for which I am relieved to know the words, but then the hand gestures start. I imitate the authoritative movements around me, many of which bear no clear relation to the text, and you descend from your lookout to investigate. When I pull you up on to my lap, you spot another abandoned bottle at the front of the room. It is made of designer stainless steel, with a distinctive paisley pattern encircling the rim. I have never before seen such a distinguished drinking utensil.

'No! Don't do it!' I cry, as you crawl beneath the chairs to the front. The song comes to an end just in time for my desperate lie: '*I've got your water bottle waiting in the car!*'

My words hang in the silent air. It is quite possible that the other mothers witnessed our arrival by bicycle. As you reach out to claim your prize, a larger blond boy snatches the bottle away, and your face crumples with injustice. I feel the same as I push through to the front, my dirty nappy bag colliding with the mothers who do not make way.

Outside, I fasten your helmet, and climb on to the bicycle behind you. Your hand is a cold clamp around my thumb; your large head bobs in front of me, nucleus of my known world. '*Go!*' you call out, though you pronounce it *doe*. Snatches of *Miss Polly Had a Dolly* issue from the swing doors, and I feel the great relief of social escape. '*Doe!*' Your tiny finger points onward, as we set off into the brilliant afternoon sky, unsocialised, and overstimulated. '*Doe!*' Yes, my darling, we are going, and we will not be coming back.

WOMBAT ROOM

Most nights, after I have extracted you from the bath and wrestled you into pyjamas and given you milk and made some gesture towards cleaning your teeth; and read you two books and then surrendered too easily and read you three; and sung through my repertoire of nursery rhymes, show tunes, out-of-season Christmas carols, half-remembered playground ditties, and improvised lullabies about moths and pirates; and extracted my hand from your grasp by kissing each of your fingers individually through the bars of your cot, and kissed the pointer finger again because your imperious point insists that I missed it; and positioned the shark by the half-opened passage door to protect you from monsters or wild boars; and turned the passage light on; and emerged into the living room for a momentary collapse on the sofa before Nicholas serves dinner, I return to the computer or the piano, ready to begin my working day.

'Trying to be Superwoman was the biggest mistake I ever made,' Baba tells me, but some evenings, buoyed by a cocktail of adrenaline and alcohol and the specific delirium that arises after a year of sleeplessness, I am able to cope. I wonder if I have cracked the code and pushed through the sleep barrier, achieving a rare enlightened state whereby I can be mother by day, career woman by night. Of course there is too much to be done, but if I work efficiently I might yet be able to reclaim that time lost – or was it time gained? – making hoovering noises by the stairwell. There is a purity to this existence, an elimination of options. I no longer bother with keeping up with friends or following current affairs, or going to concerts or parties or the cinema or the gym. There is you and then there is work. Occasionally I wave to Nicholas at his distant computer, hoping that one day we might catch up.

'You can't keep doing this,' Baba tells me. 'If you break down, the wheels come off the whole thing.'

'It's okay,' I reassure her. 'I'm coping.'

'Until one morning when suddenly you're not. Get some help.'

In the morning, I call the childcare centre once more to check your position on the waiting list. You have been enrolled since birth, but it seems that everyone else was enrolled well before conception.

'We're fine, thank you. Yes, I'm coping very well … oh, he's now number 127 on the waiting list?'

It almost feels noble: hundreds of children are pouring in ahead of you, while we chivalrously prop open the door.

'Can you stop with this *coping* thing?' Sash admonishes me. 'The worst thing you can do as a mother is *cope*.'

In fact I am not really coping. You sleep through most nights, so in theory things should be better, and yet I am more exhausted than ever. On Monday mornings, Mariah comes around to help, and I return home from teaching to find a spotless flat, in which folded laundry sits in unmolested piles on the bed, while you lie quietly on your bunny rug, leafing through *The Gruffalo*. I do not understand how this is achieved. When we are alone, you take folded laundry as a personal affront, releasing it into its natural state in the wild.

Shortly before Christmas, you take a mouthful of milk from my nipple, spit it out in disgust and never return to the breast. My milk supply dries up within the week and it is as though none of this ever happened, except for the shock of re-entry into the human world. I wake one morning to the return of sex, which until yesterday had vanished as an idea from my body.

And to anger, a deadly sin I had pondered from afar as a cow might, chewing cud, wondering why people bothered. *This is what it is to be alive*, I remind myself, *back in the seething pit of humanity.* On Christmas Day, Baba applies gel to your hair to keep it out of your eyes, without even asking. It is a violation of the purity of your scalp, an unforgivable transgression, and I have to walk for an hour along the beach before I can return to her house and look her again in the eye.

One morning, I am showering on one leg as usual, using the other foot to fling your toy car on to the bathroom tiles, in order to distract you from climbing into the toilet. Suddenly the large digger appears over the ledge, crunching into my heel, followed closely by the fluffy shark.

'Stop! That's enough!'

As I reach down to fling them out, blinded by shampoo, I feel the soft collision of your head against my ankle. You have dived in to the shower head-first, holding my new mobile phone, and all of a sudden I am shouting at you.

'Stop it! For God's sake, just *cut it out*!'

It shocks me, this loss of temper, and it shocks you too. Why the sudden fury? The cost of the phone is less significant than the enormous physical effort it took to get to the phone shop, where I pored through cryptic billing plans while you spun perilously on the stool beside me, intermittently escaping into the mall. But my frustration is deeper than that. It is the accumulated frustration of being unable to wash myself any more, unable to communicate with the outside world – at least by mobile – unable to control my temper. Together we have arrived at some new territory, some nadir of muteness, of helplessness, and for the first time since your birth I feel trapped.

As I weep with frustration, I realise that this is the ideal state in which to call the childcare centre. 'I don't know how to cope,' I tell the concerned secretary over the landline, while you bawl obligingly on my lap. 'I just feel so helpless.'

'I'll see what we can do,' she reassures me. Later that evening, when you are in bed, she phones back. By virtue of my soapy tantrum we have vaulted over 126 children to claim a place for you, two days a week. After I hang up, I give Nicholas a high five and then run from the room sobbing.

'But I thought this was what you wanted!' he calls after me.

I push open the door to your nursery, to watch you sleeping in your cot. You are still my baby; you are too young to begin your life without me. But as your brow furrows with secret dreams, already you are less knowable.

*

For your first day at the Wombat Room, Nicholas dresses you in your new t-shirt, a gift from Uncle Daniel, with rainbow-coloured letters splattered across a navy background: *Daddy's Little Monster*.

'Are you sure he should wear this?' I ask. 'Don't you think it might subliminally influence his carers?'

Together we scrutinise you, trying on the perspective of outsiders.

'Best not to risk it,' Nicholas agrees and takes you back into the nursery to change clothes. This time you emerge in a lime-green tracksuit, a hand-me-down from the neighbours. There is a danger that one of the carers might dislike lime-green, but I decide not to mention it. Downstairs, Nicholas gravely packs your nappy bag in the car, as if sending you off to war, and waves us a mournful goodbye.

'*Fwut!*' you announce, as we back out of the driveway past a truck, and the halcyon days of your infancy are returned to me: that precious first year in which you belonged only to us. It occurs to me that it is not too late, that we can skip childcare and escape to one of the playgrounds of your babyhood, but my relentless body keeps driving until we are outside the centre.

'Hello, beautiful boy!' says Pamela, letting us in. There is a lizard display by the door, a ball pit in the corner. I hand you over to her, experimentally. You settle comfortably into the pillows of her flesh, but then scrunch up the left side of your face, objecting to the process of *being handed over*.

'His disingenuous expressions are always asymmetrical,' I explain.

'Don't worry, sweetie, we'll be fine.'

There are many forms to sign: emergency numbers and medical indemnities and declarations of anaphylactic vulnerability. A baby girl starts howling, so Pamela puts you down to go comfort her. You clamber into a car by the back door and begin driving.

'Look at him – so independent,' she smiles. 'It's best if you just say a quick goodbye. But you're welcome to come back at lunch-time and check up on him.'

When I approach, you tilt your cheek up for me to kiss.

'See you later, darling.'

You raise one hand in a dismissive gesture of farewell and continue driving.

Upstairs, in the viewing room, I watch you drive away from me. Even from up here I can smell your soft, finely spun hair, I can feel the handful of curls at the bottom of your neck. There is a void on my hip where you usually sit; a cavity under my chin where you lodge your head. I knew it was a doomed intimacy, between a mother and child, a love affair in rewind: beginning with full physical communion, and moving backwards through breast and mouth and kisses and cuddles until that day when your body would no longer belong to me. But surely not so soon. Not when you are only one year old. Other babies come in and the room fills with activity. You ignore them, moving the steering wheel from left to right, expertly manoeuvring the gearstick. After half an hour's surveillance, I remove myself to a local café and spend the morning weeping over the newspaper.

At lunch-time I return and watch you through the glass pane of the front door. You are sitting on a tiny chair at a table alongside the other one-year-olds, eating vegetables and rice. It is a tableau of such civilisation and such innocence that I dare not disturb it. In the news today, Chile was hit by an earthquake; more civilians were killed in Afghanistan; a three-year-old boy went missing in Frankston. But all of it took place outside the sanctuary of this room. You catch sight of me at the door and your face lights up in welcome; then you register the glass pane between us and frown. When I come in, you stand to greet me like a gracious host and then settle back into your chair to finish your rice.

'We read a lot of books this morning,' Pamela says, 'and he could point to everything – the window, the bird, the ball. He was saying *duck*.'

I would like to remain in the Wombat Room, but soon you finish your lunch and it is time for me to go. Upstairs I watch for a while as you continue your life without me. You construct a tower from the blocks and knock it down, and then pick up a broom and sweep and sweep and sweep. It is clear that I am not, after all, necessary for your survival. You are going to be fine. I am just not sure that I am.

BREATH

Each weekend I take your childcare journal home and memorise the two days we spent apart: *He is very quiet in group activities. A gentle presence around the room. Has no special friends but enjoys playing alone.* I would not recognise my exuberant son in this, but for the photographic evidence.

'Great news!' Pamela announces, one Friday afternoon. 'He discovered the other loner today. There's a chance they might become friends.'

It is the renewal of an old sadness: I had hoped shyness was one parental legacy you might avoid. And yet when I bring you to the Wombat Room on Monday morning, you kiss me a brisk goodbye and run in laughing, ready to begin your lonely gentle play.

Until now, you have known only the things we have taught you, words passed pre-digested from our mouths to yours, like mother birds feeding their young. But now you start bringing home foreign intelligence. Pigs no longer snort, but *oink* politely. 'Uh oh,' you announce, the moment before you push over a chair. As for a good Christian, to imagine a sin is to commit it already.

One Friday you start saying *no*, and then do not stop. '*No, no, no!*' you insist, with head shake and finger waggle, as if the idea were entirely preposterous. That you might want another piece of cheese! You repeat it as a mantra in the sandpit, in your bedroom, in the back seat of the car. *No* is a much more important word than *yes*. It is a word that declares preferences, that announces the beginning of non-compliance, which is the beginning of selfhood.

There are other things you bring home from your new life. An eye swollen with conjunctivitis. An unexplained bruise on your forehead. For three Mondays in a row, a renewed bite mark on your arm.

'We have two biters in the room,' Pamela explains, 'and we're trying to monitor them both. But sometimes things slip through.'

When a bite mark appears on your face, and she asks me to sign a fourth incident report form, I have had enough. 'Why is he repeatedly the victim?'

'Part of the problem is that he's too forgiving. But we're work-shopping assertiveness.'

Back at home, Nicholas is furious. 'Who did this to you?'

'Archie!'

'I knew there was something strange about that family,' he declares. 'The way the father ponces around in those Jesus sandals.'

We glare at Archie's father for a week, but the following week you blame Ling, and then the *big girls*, and then – even less plausibly – Pamela.

Nicholas coaches you in self-defence. 'No son of mine is going to be a victim!'

'Shouldn't we encourage him to turn the other cheek?'

'Look where that's got him. Pamela said he's too forgiving. It's wombat eat wombat out there.'

He demonstrates a karate chop, and you raise your palm like a traffic cop: 'Stop! I not like it.'

'They've been workshopping assertiveness,' I explain.

*

One evening, you bring home something else. After we have put you to bed and sat down at our computers, we hear a foreign noise from your room: a dry phocine bark. When I check on you in the nursery, you are asleep, but your bottom lip and jaw jut out with each cough, as if seeking to turn your mouth inside out.

Baby barking like a seal, Nicholas types into Google.

Your child probably has croup. Croup can develop from a harmless cough to a life-endangering condition very quickly, so be sure to remain vigilant. If baby struggles to breathe or his lips turn blue, call emergency services immediately.

I phone Baba and bring the phone into the nursery where she confirms Google's diagnosis. 'Try steam if it gets worse. But if he develops stridor – that high-pitched crowing sound on the inhalation – get him to the hospital straightaway.'

So here we are again, back up against the fact of your mortality. I take up a sentry post on the beanbag beside your cot and listen to you cough. It is a more effortful cough than before; it has larger designs on your larynx, on your chest, and soon it wakes you up. The more it possesses you, the more you cry, and the more you cry, the more you struggle to breathe. I take you into the bathroom and turn on the shower. 'Tap!' you announce, applauding yourself, but then you register the wrongness of this scenario and start howling, your chest wall veering inwards on each intake. The only thing that consoles you is the electric toothbrush, and as we sit on the toilet lid you buzz it on and off, while around us the bathroom fills with steam.

Once your breath has relaxed, I bring you into bed with me so that my body can monitor you while I sleep, though of course I will not sleep. I have again lost my nerve: your ongoing existence is improbable once more, subject to the co-operation of too many small parts. When the cough gets worse, you start bawling. You are too little for this cough; it possesses your body entirely. There is no bolthole, no escape: everything is right here, foreground. I wish I could explain illness to you, explain that there will be an after, but by the time you have coughed for three hours I can no longer explain this to myself. My world has contracted not just to your breathing, but to this breath, and now this one, and now the one that comes next. As I spoon your feverish body, you spoon the toothbrush, switching it on and off.

Towards midnight, Nicholas climbs into the vibrating bed: 'You've got to be joking.' I try to nudge the toothbrush from your hands but you clasp your fingers around it more tightly, until the three of us settle into a rhythm: *cough, sob, vibrate.*

Sometime overnight the dog makes a curious noise in the corner, a stifled hiccup, and for a moment I wish all illness upon him – wish the lightning to strike over there, instead – but then he is silent again. All night you cough like a reproach. I come to hate your cough. I hate it. In my midnight derangement I can hear death in it. Compulsively, I revise the emergency checklist: the location of my glasses, the car keys, your blanket; the route we would take to the hospital.

Early in the morning you pause to lick your lips. When I offer you water, you gurgle towards me with open mouth. I reach forward with cupped hands, but your vomit spills over them, until we are both drenched in regurgitated tuna and milk and bile.

'Good thing we had him in bed with us,' I say, as Nicholas turns on the light.

'I don't follow.'

You are always delighted after throwing up – lighter, renewed – and as I sponge you down in the bathroom, you throw yourself on the tiles, kicking your legs in the air in a break-dancing move usually reserved for visitors, until your cough forces you to stop. We return to bed and I turn you on to your side, checking your breathing with my hand on your chest, listening out for any signs of wheeze or stridor. Sometimes the cough stops, and sleep beckons like music: a place innocent of maternal fear, a place where all will be well. But my script is this: *Do not let yourself imagine it will be okay. For your complacency you will be punished.* Your inhalations and exhalations – clouded with phlegm, with the softest whistle or snore – are my only reality; your breath the air on which I construct my existence. Part of me flirts with sleep, but there is another part, bone old, lizard still, that remains awake, watching you. It is a supervisory self, ancient as the species. I watch you with my skin, with my blood, with my breath, tracking the safe passage of your breath – in and out, in and out – until it carries us to morning.

*

By the third night, your cough has loosened and become human; by the fifth night, you scarcely cough at all. Early in the morning you start speaking in tongues, seizing my head and broadcasting into my ear: '*Dumblefy biggles!*' I am not sure if this is funny or if it is the tickle of your warm breath that makes me laugh.

'Both of you be quiet!' scolds Nicholas.

Your large eyes stare at the ceiling, catching the early morning light; I can hear the ticking industry of your head. When I try to soothe you with a nursery rhyme, you reward me with rousing applause. At dawn, you start shouting declarations before even opening your eyes, pretending you had not been asleep on the job. '*Thnot!*' you pronounce through your nose, as though snot itself were talking, and I sit up to wipe your nose and begin our day, eager to believe in normality.

It is a faith I continue to cultivate as we ride to childcare that morning. You cough once at the traffic lights, but it is too isolated to be taken seriously. Shortly after lunch, I receive a stern phone call from Pamela: 'He's been coughing very strangely in the nap room. You have to collect him immediately.'

I abandon my student and rush to childcare, where I find you quarantined on the back porch. The shame of it. Sending a sick child to childcare. Imperilling the other children. Pamela sees us out and hovers at the door to make sure we leave. 'Don't come back without a doctor's certificate.'

At the local health care clinic, you are gleeful with truancy. The doctor calls us in, and you address yourself to his rubbish bin, pushing the foot pedal so that it claps open and shut.

'Detain that child,' he commands. He is tall and florid, with combed-over white hair, and sits in front of a large bookshelf, as custodian of all its knowledge. 'Where are you from?'

'Adelaide, originally.' You attempt to escape my lap, so I hold you tighter.

'Adelaide!' he snorts as if it were funny, or telling. 'Adelaide, of course, is where they harbour Thinkers-in-Residence. I've always thought I should be a Thinker-in-Residence.'

It is important to establish rapport with this doctor and thereby fix this day. But my timid laughter is not the correct response.

'You can dismiss what I'm saying, if you like. But I'll have you know I've done more than twenty years of research.'

'What sort of research?'

'Research on *oils*.'

'How interesting.' I am still seeking the universe's forgiveness for sending a sick child to childcare. 'What sort of oils?'

He studies my face, before deciding I do not deserve to hear any more. 'Why are you here, exactly?'

'I think my son is recovering from croup.'

'That's for me to say, not you.' He pulls out his stethoscope and listens perfunctorily to your chest. 'No croup there.'

Released from examination, you run to the bookshelf, where a model of a heart teeters like a ripe piece of fruit.

'That's not a toy,' I warn you.

The doctor passes me a prescription and then glares over his half-moon glasses. 'I will ask you again to detain that child. I have something important to tell you about him.'

I quickly retrieve you, eager to hear important things about my favourite subject.

'You may not be aware of this, but I have made a number of observations since you came into the room. Number one: this is a very active child.'

'He's certainly very curious.' This is as far as I will allow myself to boast; curious being a code word for so much more.

'I've seen this sort of child before, though rarely around these parts. Much more common in the western suburbs, to tell you the truth. Now answer the following questions, to the best of your ability. I note the sunglasses resting on your head. You're very sensitive to light, correct?'

'We came on the bike. It is a bright afternoon.'

'Indeed. And tell me, have you been having problems with short-term memory?'

'A little, since I gave up sleeping a couple of years ago.'

There is a satisfied cluck. 'I've spent the last twenty years researching this. Believe me, I know what I'm talking about.

When children are this active, it can mean one of two things. It can mean they're very intelligent, though in this case that's unlikely. Winston Churchill was an example of this type of child – have you heard of him?'

'Of course.' I hope my command of British history will sway him towards the first diagnosis.

'But there's a much more likely explanation. I have reason to believe your son lacks impulse control. Correct?'

'I suppose. But he's only ...'

'Didn't I say I knew what I was talking about? And how would you rate his road sense?'

Are one-year-olds supposed to have good road sense? Is this something else I have neglected in your upbringing?

'You don't need to answer. I can see that I'm spot-on.' He scans over our notes, raising the deductive finger of a master detective. 'I observe you live in a university residential college. Every college, with the exception of St Hilda's, is churning out students who wear sunglasses day and night and who repeatedly fail their law exams, because of their lack of short-term memory!'

I try to discern the connection between your cough and these amnesiac law students in dark glasses. 'Why?'

'Because college cafeterias cook with hydrolysed vegetable oils!'

'But we cook for ourselves ... '

'Yes, but I bet that you don't check what oils they use when you go into a restaurant, do you?'

'But ... '

'I'll tell you what your favourite restaurants are cooking with. Hydrolysed vegetable oil, or canola. It depletes the body of Vitamin E, meaning your son has a greater chance of developing Alzheimer's later in life. All part of the profile.'

'I'm sorry. What exactly are you saying?'

'I'm telling you that your son has Attention Deficit Disorder.'

He stares at me with vindicated pinkish eyes. I am so astonished that I do not know what to say. 'Thank you. That's very interesting information.'

We leave the room and I pay the bill. It is only when we cross the road and get to the playground that I realise I am outraged enough to call Baba.

'The man's a hazard! Why the hell did you sit there and listen to that rubbish?'

'He was the doctor.'

'What did you say to him?'

I cannot bring myself to confess that I thanked him. 'Nothing, really.'

'What would he know after five minutes' observation?'

'That he's active and lacks impulse control, apparently.'

'For God's sake, that's just the definition of a *boy*. You need to report that idiot before he does more damage.'

Baba's outrage rights things a little. I agree that I might lodge a complaint, though I do not really believe I will. After I hang up, I realise I forgot to ask for a doctor's certificate, but I will not be going back. Instead I take the remainder of the week off work. The following Monday, you still lack road sense and impulse control, but all traces of a cough have disappeared, and nobody at the Wombat Room remembers to ask.

SNAKES AND SNAILS

It is curious to hear Baba explain you as a boy. Baba, who never believed in gender difference. Who banned Barbie dolls from our childhood home, supplying me instead with Tonka trucks; who reprimanded shopkeepers for calling her *love*, insisting they address her as *sir*. When I was six, I convinced her to buy me a board game set in an office. Its orderliness pleased me – a handful of bluff, hearty executives presiding over a pool of dimpled secretaries – but at home she took the scissors to the name tags, promoting all the secretaries into executives and relegating the executives to the typing pool. *That's taking this women's lib business a little far*, my great-grandmother remarked, and silently I agreed. Baba was studying to be a doctor, but I told everyone at school that she was a nurse.

'Motherhood cured me of my idealistic beliefs,' she says now. 'Boys and girls are different species.'

It saddens me that she has abandoned her campaign. 'But you were only operating from a sample of three. I might not have liked trucks, but I'm sure you did.'

'True.'

'So what species does that make you?'

This cheers her up. 'Good question.'

But it is clear that you, too, are a foreign species. Before you were born, I had imagined you as something pale and contemplative, the natural progeny of Nicholas and myself. Instead you are tawny, athletic and *very active*, as the doctor correctly identified, the true heir to those Tonka trucks, arriving a generation too late. Is this a delayed expression of the Baba gene, or is she right and you are *just a boy*?

'There's no intrinsic difference between boys and girls,' Fiona maintains over brunch. 'It's all conditioning.'

You bite the edges off your toast until you have turned it into a gun: 'BANG!'

From the way Fiona recoils, I can tell she has never previously been shot by a piece of bread.

'How am I conditioning that, exactly?'

'Subconsciously. On some level, you are gratified by the myth of gender difference. Without realising it, you are coaching him in masculinity.'

It is true that there is an emotional totalitarianism to motherhood: I not only name things, but tell you what to think about them. But already you are a dissenting voice.

'I want to pick your nose and eat your snot.'

'I don't think you should do that. Snot is yucky.'

'No, Mummy. SNOT IS YUMMY!'

Every evening before bed, Nicholas attempts his own conditioning. 'Concentrate for a moment. This is how a cuddle works. You put one arm around here and another arm here.'

You try for a moment and become impatient – where is the impact, the explosion, the hilarious surprise? Then you brace your legs against his torso and eject to freedom.

'Cuddles are what we pay you for!' he calls as you disappear into the living room, where you are remaking the sofa into a pirate ship.

Despite my best efforts, I start dividing mothers into two species also. At the playground, some women are able to sit and talk, while their daughters play shop with wood chips. Meanwhile, I trace laps around the perimeter, smiling wryly at the mothers of other little boys on the way past. Probably our days together are fun; probably I will look back on them and recognise them as happiness. But it is so difficult to see you: you are forever in motion. Perhaps this is why people drug their children with Ritalin, or park them in front of screens. Sometimes I gaze on your face during your afternoon nap, pinned by sleep like a butterfly against a board, and I gasp at your beauty. *I've hit paydirt. This trumps everything.*

When it is time for your first haircut, the hairdresser goes too far, shedding your baby curls until you are as shorn as a marine. 'What have you done?' Nicholas asks, a little tearfully, but I do not mind. I have better access to your scalp this way, to its smell and texture. There is something greedy about mother love. Occasionally I check your nappy even when I do not have to, for a glimpse of your bottom, secret and peachy and self-possessed. When tidying up, I inhale your discarded clothes for those smells that announce your quiet claim on the world: soap, Vegemite, boy. Snakes and snails and puppy dog tails.

Do I love you differently than I would a daughter? Many years ago, a woman tried to persuade me to teach piano to her adolescent son: 'He's a *young stallion*,' she had breathed over the phone. I had thought it unseemly and changed the subject. But now I find myself moved by your incipient masculinity. By your husky voice; by the strength and warmth of your small hands. Even by the way you bellow at me from your high chair, waving your sippy cup like a male chauvinist: 'MORE!' One morning in the shower, I catch a glimpse of the boy you will become: your cherub's body unfolded into something elongated and beautiful.

As I spend more time in your head each day, I begin to wonder who is conditioning whom. Motherhood is all empathy: from the cretinous way I open my mouth while slipping a spoon into yours; to the delight I now take in the existence of diggers; to the anticipatory pleasure of needing to fart, as before delivering a one-liner of great wit. Perhaps you have succeeded in conditioning me where Baba failed. I am becoming more boy.

WORDS

Shortly before you turned one, you casually revealed you knew everything.

'Where's the light? The sky? The light *switch*?'

You pointed offhandedly at each item and continued playing. I was astonished by this secret stash of knowledge. All of this time when you were pretending to be a baby – mute, oblivious – you were quietly swotting the world, collecting language by stealth.

I pressed you further: 'Who do I love?'

You tapped yourself once on the chest and returned to your blocks.

When you began attending the Wombat Room, you only had two words: 'ball' for ball, and 'a-dya' for anything remarkable. The two categories were not mutually exclusive: balls were the ultimate manifestation of 'a-dya.' But now you collect more and more words, importing them into your head in order of importance – dog, fan, piano, water, truck. How it thrills me to hear you name things, to have their existence confirmed! With each new word you acquire, the shared space of our personhood expands, a place that now includes the moon and shoes and the vacuum cleaner and your nose.

'But all he ever says is *ball*!' says Fiona, tone-deaf to the nuances of your vowels, to the subtle difference between *boo* for moon and *boo* for shoe. How wrong she is! *Mroaar* indicates thirst; a *dyul*, pronounced slightly mournfully, is a helicopter. I do not understand why you call me *Ba*, until one afternoon you pick up the phone and impersonate my phone manner, complete with dotty upward inflection – '*Ba?*' – and I realise you have named me in the same way you have named the farmyard animals, after their snorts and bleats. Such a system makes good sense, but I long to hear you say *Mummy*. I know you can say it: I have overheard you mumbling it to yourself in the nursery. Meanwhile, you shower Nicholas with praise every evening when he returns home from work: 'Dadadada!'

How can anyone truly learn a second language? Because you are not only learning language, you are learning the world, and surely this can only be done once. There is a giraffe on your quilt and another in your book: a *same-same*! *Same-sames* are cause for jubilation. They are the building blocks of meaning, each offering the fizz of a new cognitive pathway. Sitting in the car at a traffic light, we watch a young boy totter past with his mother. You press forward in your seat – 'boy!' – and point back at yourself – 'boy!' In your pleased grin I witness the dawn of self-knowledge.

At the children's farm, you take out your picture book to instruct the cow in her likeness. She feigns a polite interest and then moves along to a little girl who offers grass instead of literature. In the guinea-pig enclosure, an older girl places a guinea-pig on your lap, but you are too mesmerised by the red ribbon in her hair to notice. When you glance down at your lap, you discover a pile of quivering fur. 'GOAT!' you exclaim. Everything is either question or exclamation; sometimes I crave the repose of a full stop.

Early in the new year, I spend a week away for work, and discover to my heartbreak that it is possible to live without you. Every day your likeness recedes like a dream. Nicholas's image, entrenched in adult identity, remains much more vivid. So I try to remember you through your words. The way you call out *boob* after an injury: although my breasts no longer belong to you, you retain some memory of their significance. The reverential way you pronounce the word *play* upon sighting a playground, cradling the word in your mouth like a crush. The humourlessness of all matters pertaining to *bottle*.

I reconstruct you in my mind as a fully verbal human being and am surprised on my return to discover that you are still a baby, making baby talk. A shower is a *shuff*, rhyming with *buff* for butterfly. Later, when dragonflies become perfectly enunciated dragonflies, buffs continue their sturdy flight around our backyard. Many of your words are improvements: *rhine-horse* for rhinoceros, *last-today* for yesterday. 'Matilda is a *naughtle*!' you tell me in scandalised tones, after she messes up your bedroom.

When you rename the dog *Lupple*, I campaign to make it official, but Nicholas resists: 'There's no way I'm shouting that in the dog park.'

Soon you start joining words together in small sentences, experimental as Duplo constructions. 'Lupple did a wee in the shuff,' you tell me, and I transcribe this small poem – this perfect synthesis of meaning and expression – into my notebook even before I clean up the mess. For a time, it seems language might tame you, that the pleasure of obeying an understood command might override that of mischief. 'Chairs are for sitting down on, not for climbing,' I tell you, and when you sit down it is with great mastery over both word and thing. But language also offers further possibilities for subversion. 'What's that?' I ask, pointing at the dragonfly in your picture book.

'Poo!' you grin.

'Then what's that?' I point at a moth.

'POO!'

'Don't push him to talk before he's ready,' Mariah says. 'He's still little.'

'I not little. I a *naughtle*!' you correct her, and run off giggling.

In October, we travel to New York. The city subdues you, and you sit wide-eyed in your pusher, making the occasional sage declaration: 'Big money!' In Greenwich Village, we paint pumpkins for Halloween, as skulls leer at us from shop windows and lynched dummies dangle from balconies. Afterwards, we walk back to our apartment past Ground Zero.

'Man fall!' you inform us, grimly.

'Did you show him footage?' Nicholas whispers.

'Course not.'

'Unless it was the Wombat Room?'

'Surely they couldn't have?'

In Central Park, you run towards the sandpit, to join an older blond boy playing with two plastic horses.

'Neigh!' you venture, with the broad diphthong of an Australian horse.

He places his horses down and looks at you. 'I'm sorry, but I just don't follow.'

'Neigh!' you repeat.

'I'm not catching your meaning.'

Somehow, the two of you arrive at an international understanding. When a third boy requests to join the game, the blond boy politely declines – 'I already have my horse and my friend' – and you improvise a dance routine in the sand, with your arm jutting backwards, fingers ecstatically splayed.

On the weekend I fly to Canada for work. The only solution to missing you is not thinking of you, but not thinking of you becomes its own heartbreak. I pretend that I am getting away with all this busyness, but I am not really. The price is these two black bags under my eyes; the price is your evaporating babyhood. But when you come to meet me at the airport, you call me *Mum* for the first time, and everything is mended.

*

Back home in Melbourne, it is time for your two-year check-up at the Family Health Centre.

'How old are you?' asks Nurse Fran.

You get that pleased, cunning look I know from Pop, advance notice of an approaching witticism. 'Yellow!'

I sigh, wishing you would indulge me.

'How is his comprehension generally?' she asks.

'Excellent.'

She raises a sceptical eyebrow. 'Okay, my friend, since you like colours so much, perhaps you can tell me what colour this one is?'

'Blue.' It is a small triumph of co-operation.

'And this?'

'Dreen.' I hope she does not notice you cannot pronounce your Gs. She pulls out an orange swatch. 'And here's a difficult one. What is it?'

'Nonta.'

'Exactly!' I applaud.

'I'm sorry. I didn't realise you were raising him to be bilingual.'

For a second I wonder if we can maintain this fiction, earning you extra points for giftedness, but I glance a few moves ahead and discard the idea. 'Only in the sense that he speaks English and a language of his own invention.'

'I see.' She writes something in her notes. 'And are you the only person who understands him?'

'Oh no. Lots of people do.'

She pulls out a picture on a card. 'What's this?'

'A dod.'

'Do you have a dog?'

'Less.'

'And what's the dog's name?'

'Lupple.'

She looks at me. 'What sort of name is that?'

'A family name,' I improvise.

'Is that right? How do you spell it?'

I attempt the Scandinavian variant – 'L-U-P-P-E-L' – all the while wondering how I came to be in this place, inventing a pretend spelling of a dog's pretend name for a nurse. When it is time to leave, she suggests I speak and read to you more, to foster your language development. I consider arguing – *but that's the only thing I do* – but decide not to. Perhaps the experts are becoming less important.

Outside, I fasten your helmet, and climb on to my bike. I can feel the edges of the blue book in my backpack in which your language skills have been declared *fair*.

Have you countenanced the possibility that your baby might not be a genius? I was once asked, before you were born. *It doesn't matter who or what our baby is*, I replied, imagining I could protect you from my ambition. But now I see that the question is redundant.

It doesn't matter who or what our baby is, you will be a genius anyway.

HORSE

At first I had the fantasy that I might only teach you the words of good things. What you did not know – what we never activated through language – would never need to exist in your life. And so I read you stories about possums and kittens and bunny rabbits, reassurance to myself as much as to you that this was a safe world, a world of fluffy animals and pastel colours, an appropriate place for raising a baby.

One evening you selected a Beatrix Potter story from the bookcase that we had not yet read. It was about a fierce, bad rabbit who did not know how to share; perhaps this could be the limit of evil in your universe. But when we turned the page, a hunter unexpectedly appeared with a gun. 'BANG!'

You sat up. 'What that?'

'Just a gun.' I tried to turn to the next page, but you would not let me.

'Bang!' you said, experimentally. 'BANG BANG BANG!' There was a gleeful recognition to it. And every night for weeks, your book choice remained the same: 'BANG BANG BANG!'

As you grow older, there are other stories you come to love. Dr Seuss, which I resist because our life already feels Dr Seuss enough. There is already a fox in a box, a fish in a tree; or at least a sock in the dishwasher, a dinosaur in the teapot. I crave order in your stories, not further hallucinogenic reality. But you are drawn to its rhymes:

I would not eat green eggs and ham.
I do not like them Sam-I-Am.

Soon you begin inventing your own rhymes: 'I would not eat green eggs and *pam*! Is that funny?'

'Sort of.'

'Then could you please laugh?'

Pop visits and provides us with new stories, sketching cartoons on a sheet of paper. He begins with your likeness, all giant eyes and tiny body, accessorised with the dog. In the first panel, the two of you set off on an adventure, while Nicholas and I wave goodbye from the front door.

'You know he tried to let himself out the front door,' I whisper. 'To go to the airport.'

'I think he understands it's pretend,' Pop says. 'Don't you?'

You nod gravely and he continues. One day, you go to the beach and are captured by a pirate's giant butterfly net. Another day, you meet a wild boar in a forest and produce a pencil sharpener from your pocket to sharpen his tusks. Each story offers a small narrative of reassurance – the intrusion of chaos and then the restoration of order – and concludes with you returning home to our welcoming silhouettes at the front door.

After Pop has gone back to Adelaide, you take your cartoons into your cot every night, bringing them into bed with us in the morning for further analysis.

'Careful!' you warn me, as I unravel them, crumpled from another night of co-sleeping. You are very proud of your resourcefulness in these stories. 'I had a good idea! I took the big big big pirate hat and threw it into the sea upside down and turned it into a boat.'

I recognise the narcissistic thrill of these cartoons, in which you are the acknowledged hero of your own life. It is a thrill I remember from my own childhood, when Pop began each cartoon with one of my pigtails and then the other, and the story grew outwards from there.

'Did that really happen?' I ask. 'Or is it just pretend?'

You study my face for the right answer, fiction and memory already blurred.

'Maybe it was a dream,' you offer.

*

In the new year, we move into a house with a backyard, so that you no longer need a chaperone to play outside. You let yourself out through the back door and sit for hours in the sandpit, baking cupcakes, herding wild boars, rescuing pirate ships from icebergs. Vestiges of autonomy return for me too. It becomes possible to cook decent meals, to clean the kitchen, stepping outside only at intervals to dispense applause.

Early one evening, shortly after Nicholas has returned from work, there is a terrified scream from the sandpit. It is a sound we have not heard from you before – mortal fear – and as we jump up, you hurtle through the back door and fling yourself into Nicholas's arms.

'What's wrong? Did you hurt yourself?'

You weep grievously, incoherent with terror, and it is some time before you can breathe out a single word: 'Horse.'

We venture outside to investigate, and you continue to sob, your face wedged into Nicholas's armpit.

'Where was the horse, darling?'

Your blind, outstretched finger points to nothing and we glance at each other, perplexed. Then we hear a snort from the fence and turn to look. A large round hole in the wood. And pressed up against it, a huge unblinking eye. You had thought you were playing alone, but all along you were being watched.

'Shoo!' scolds Nicholas, and a boxer detaches itself from the fence, lolloping back to the neighbour's deck. 'It was just a funny dog. He wanted to look at the pirate ship you were making.'

'Horse,' you continue to weep. 'Horse.'

I had hoped to spare you the horse, as I had hoped to spare you the fox in the henhouse, the wolf in the forest, all the great monsters of the night. But of course none of us can escape the horse and its gimlet eye.

A week later I return home to wild laughter. You are chasing the baby-sitter around the house with the stuffed shark: that giant fearsome *roaring* fish.

'My turn,' she says. 'Watch out! The monster is coming to get you!'

The laughter evaporates from your face and your eyes grow very large. 'Where's the monster?'

She glances at me. 'Did I say monster? I meant shark. There's no monster in this house.'

You run towards me and clamber into my arms. 'Is there a monster outside?'

'Definitely not! We would never allow a monster near our house.'

But that night at story-time, you can hear a monster breathing in the oil heater.

'No, darling. That's just the oil heating up. No monsters will ever come to our house.'

I select *Where the Wild Things Are* from your bookshelf. It is one of your favourites, a story I have caught you re-enacting several times, as you chase the dog down the passage with a fork. But tonight you shake your head and push it away – 'Better put that one away, Mummy. It might frighten me' – and ask to read *Miss Moppet* instead.

One night when I was only a few years older than you, Pop told me a different sort of story. He arranged my favourite glass ornaments at the edge of the mantelpiece: a transparent glass bird with bubbles in it, alongside its brown glass companion, brought back from Venice by my grandparents.

The transparent bird wobbled to the ledge and peeked over. 'I've had enough. I'm going to jump!'

Pop gathered my stuffed toys on the carpet below and began a chant: 'Jump. Jump. Jump.'

I did not understand. 'They should tell him to stop.'

'No. They want to see him jump.'

'Jump!' the soft toys continued. 'Jump, jump, jump!'

They were all soft toys. None of them was made of glass. I looked around for Superman, or the fireman with the giant trampoline, but nobody came and the bird jumped.

'*Splat.*'

The crowd rushed in to look: 'Hip hip hooray!'

This was not right. 'Why are they cheering?'

'Because some people love the sight of blood.'

'Why?'

He grinned, and his grin confused me. 'Because that's the way the world is.'

I had to act as if this did not trouble me. Otherwise there would be no further confidences, no further revelations about the adult world. Now I wonder: why did he tell me such a story? Was it sport? Or an attempt at vaccination, at exposing me to small, controllable quantities of evil, the better to build up my resistance?

Nicholas buys you a volume of fairy tales, and you are enchanted by their songs, by their rhythms – *Fee fi fo fum, I smell the blood of an Englishman!* Then the questions begin.

'Why is Jack hiding in the copper pot?'

'Because the giant is coming home.'

'Why he not want the giant to see him?'

I hesitate. 'Because the giant likes to eat children.'

'Why?'

'He thinks they are yummy.'

The back of your neck becomes very still, and I wonder if I have gone too far. 'Tell me that again.'

'That silly giant likes to eat children.'

'NO!' There is such reprimand in the way you say it that I feel I should apologise. 'Giants don't eat *children*.'

You set the word *children* down sacredly, as if this concept is as unbearable to you as it is to me. That things are done to children.

'Nobody eats children. You don't eat children.'

'Maybe not,' I backtrack. 'And anyway, giants are just pretend.'

'I don't eat me,' you continue, as if explaining this to a simple-minded person. 'See!' You pretend to bite your arm as proof.

'No, of course not. Children are not for eating. You're right.'

And we both laugh with relief.

But later that night, you wake screaming in your cot. When I run into your nursery, your screams give way to giant gulping sobs. 'DON'T EAT!'

'It's okay,' I shush you.

'NO!'

'It was just a made-up story. Giants are just pretend. Like monsters.'

There are other things that are not pretend, but you do not need to know about them just yet. After a while your sobs subside and I place you back in your cot, and it is silent in your room apart from the monster breathing in your heater.

'Leave the shark by the door,' you murmur as I leave.

Back in bed, I tell Nicholas that you had a nightmare. 'I think it might be my fault.'

'Why?'

For some reason I am smiling. 'I told him that giants like to eat children.'

He shoots me an unusually judgemental look. 'You know how scared he is of monsters. Why on *earth* would you do that?'

Was it just vaccination, or was it something else: an attempt to work it out better for myself? As if I could make better sense of evil by seeing it refracted through your soft features?

'You're the one who bought him the fairy tales.'

'Yes, but you don't need to terrify him with every grisly detail. That's just bad parenting.'

He switches off the light like a reprimand. My t-shirt is still damp with your tears, and yet I continue to grin into the dark. It is a grin I remember as Pop's grin, after the suicide of the glass bird: the grin of the bearer of bad news. *Because that's the way the world is.* It is sheepish and shamefaced, but also a little glad. Because it is better, after all, that you know.

PIRATES

Already you are two and a half years old. In December, you plan to turn three and a half years old.

'And what are you going to be when you grow up?' asks Baba.

'A big scary rabbit with sharp teeth. And frighten you!'

She screams in alarm; you cackle like a criminal mastermind. We are in Adelaide for the long weekend and have crammed in visits to Pop, Sash and Daniel, who has moved back, to your two young cousins, your three great-grandparents. On the final day, we go to see Great-Grandma Moggy.

'I not want to see Moggy. I not like it.'

When I was a child I had four great-grandmothers, each with a different shade of mauve hair, along with a single bald great-grandfather. Every weekend we visited a nursing home, and I was forced to kiss a crepey cheek. I did not like it, either.

'But Moggy will be so happy to see you. Then we'll go to the art gallery and look at that exhibition Pop told you about.'

'What exhibition?'

'Funny statues.'

When we arrive at Moggy's house, we let ourselves in the open front door. I grasp your hand tightly as we move through the living room, past its lifetime collection of ornaments and antiques. There is an elderly man in the kitchen wearing a plaid dressing gown. He stares at us, disoriented, and for a moment I fear that we have stepped into the wrong house. Then I recognise Moggy's companion, Bob. He has not yet put his hearing aid in, and is puffy, confused, a stranger.

Moggy waits for us in the sunroom, dressed in a cashmere cardigan and slacks, with a set of jade beads slung around her neck. She is perfectly made-up, but she is wearing her ugg boots.

'I couldn't get me socks on this morning,' she confesses as I hug her.

This is the last time you will see her, I am sure of it. And then you will not remember her. You kiss her robustly, and climb on to the chair opposite to sing *Puff the Magic Dragon*. At the end of every verse you tilt your face up to her, to the sunshine of her praise. 'What a boy, what a boy,' she chuckles.

Bob shuffles in and lobs a foam ball at you, and you return it. After three throws he is wheezing and sits down, grasping at his chest. Surrounded by a captive audience, you launch into a break-dancing routine on the carpet, and then attempt a backward somersault. Your acrobatics make me nervous. There are too many breakable things in this room: the glass epergne, the Worcester plates. Bob. Moggy.

'How are you feeling, Moggy?'

'Fine within myself, dear, but weak as a cat.'

Last time I visited, she had started a course of quantum healing and made me promise not to tell Baba. 'I'll let her know if I come up trumps!'

But this time there is no talk of coming up trumps. She is fretful about global warming, sorry that she has not told me enough of her stories. 'It's too late, it's just too late.'

'But you've told me hundreds of your stories.'

'I never could properly express what Mother was like. The children never knew her at her best, you see.'

I realise she fears her mother will die with her, and I scan my mind for memories. 'You said she was a woman of great dignity. A most efficient woman. You said she always had the cleanest house and the whitest whites.'

'Is this a trampoline or a bounce-aline?' you ask, climbing on to the grandfather chair.

'Neither. It's for sitting on.'

'And is it for jumping on as well?'

'No!' In desperation I hand you my phone. You navigate it expertly, finding a loud Spanish cartoon on YouTube.

'She used to play *Rigoletto* on the piano,' I continue, 'when you were in bed. She hated flies and hardly ever sat down. Every morning she filled a gravy boat with cream from the stove.'

'Even so, even so. I was never able to do her justice with my words. She had the most beautiful laugh. A beautiful contralto laugh.'

'*Canastos! Desgraciado de él!*'

'What's going on over there, then?' Bob blinks.

I reach over and turn the volume down on the phone.

'No, Mummy. I not want you to do that.'

'I just never had that gift, to express myself in words. Not like some people. Not like my friend Roma. She was born in early June, same as you. The thirteenth star sign, you see.'

'I not want you to turn volume down, Mummy.'

'Be quiet, please. I'm talking to Moggy.'

'I want to see some funny statues!'

I realise this visit will shortly come to an end, so I go into Moggy's bedroom to fetch her socks. They are lying on a foot stool, abandoned next to her shoes, and I bring them back to the sunroom and pull them over her pale feet. Your feet resisted capture this morning, but Moggy's are more compliant, as I coax on her shoes and tighten the laces.

'Lovely girl,' she murmurs, stroking my hair.

'You're a good girl, you are,' pipes up Bob.

It seems important not to cry.

'I want to go. I want to see some funny statues!'

'I think we're going to have to make tracks,' I tell Moggy.

'Already?' She eases herself up to her walking frame. Standing up, she is reed thin, semi-transparent. Bob shuffles to his feet and hugs me vigorously. At the door, the winter sun filters through her fine auburn hair, lights her skin from inside. You give her a final kiss goodbye, a kiss into oblivion – 'Bye, Moggy!' – and then run to the car and climb into your baby seat.

As we back out the driveway and turn down the crescent, I see her silhouette behind the security door. She is still waving as we drive off.

'We going to see some funny statues now, Mummy?'

How soon we are erased.

*

A week later we are in Port Fairy on the Victorian coast. After books and lullabies, I turn off the light and hold your hand through the slats in the cot.

'What's going to happen when I turn seven? Will I be a man?'

'No. You won't be a man until you're about twenty. When you grow up.'

'And when I grow up, you will get little again?'

Sometimes I think we share the same cosmology, and then I realise we do not. 'I might shrink a little bit, but I hope not too much.'

'And I can pick you up?'

'Probably, because you'll be big by then.'

'And when you was a baby, I was bigger than you?'

'What do you mean?'

'I could look after you.'

It is a charming notion, you and me alternating through eternity, bringing each other up. I am not sure I wish to disabuse you of it. But I have resolved to try to tell you the truth about things. 'No, darling. When I was a baby, you weren't even born yet.'

'What does not born mean?'

'It means you hadn't even started.'

'What?'

'Your life hadn't begun. You weren't a person yet.'

There is a long silence in which you contemplate this. Then you release my hand and pull a blanket over your head – 'Goodnight, Mummy' – and I feel as if I have informed you of your death.

The following morning, you wake early with a croup: that tight, focused bark on every exhalation. I wrap you in a blanket and carry you outside into the winter morning. We cross the road away from the hotel and sit on a bench outside the art gallery. You are still warm with sleep, a giant white grub in your sleeping bag, and I wrap my arms around you, breathing into your hair, feeling your breath against my chest until the moist night air loosens your cough, and the croup subsides. An early-rising magpie starts up, and a lone light comes on in the hotel kitchen. Together we gaze up at the brightening sky.

'There's the moon,' you rasp, and discover you have lost your voice. You turn to me in wonder. 'I a *pirate*!'

The day is strangely silent without your questions. We take you to a doctor, who prescribes steroids, and then wander along the boardwalk to the lighthouse, swinging you between us. As we pass a replica Portuguese ship, the shipbuilder steps off and sets up an open sign. He is wiry and weather-beaten, with scraggy hair.

'A pirate!' you whisper, in awe.

I am feeling nauseous and remain on shore as you and Nicholas climb to the top deck to gaze out at the ocean. Your face is puffy with illness, your snot glistens in the sun, but you grin back at me in mute rapture.

Back at the hotel, Baba calls to say Moggy has gone into a hospice. When I phone her, her voice is a frail peep, a baby bird's. 'I foolishly overdid it yesterday. I tried to put things in order at home.'

'I hope a bit of rest makes you feel better.'

'It will, darling. But I'm not sure that it's a question of making a full recovery.'

She says this tentatively. I am not sure if she hopes to be mistaken, or if is she is trying to protect me from the truth.

It is difficult to sleep that night. I lie awake listening to your cough like a connoisseur, gauging its density, its dryness. The second night is usually the worst, but surely the steroids will start working soon. At midnight, I bring you into bed with us. You thrash around beneath the covers, swimming laps of the bed, wedging yourself between the pillows and the headboard. I do not mind. At least I know you are breathing.

The following day they are no longer putting calls through to Moggy's room, so we drive back to Melbourne in the late afternoon, through the dark and the rain. Your voice has returned, and with it the questions.

'Is it a day? Is it a beautiful day?'

'It's a day, but not a very beautiful one.'

'Is a grandpa a type of big thing?'

'As big as Pop.'

'Is a crow a bit like a snowman?'

'Not at all.' (It will only be four hours of answering questions. Surely we can manage this.)

'What I am saying now?'

'You're asking me what you're saying now.'

'And what you are saying?'

'I'm telling you what you're saying.'

'What you are telling me?'

(An SUV appears over the crest, blinding us with its headlights.)

Nicholas clutches the steering wheel. 'Turn off your high-beams, dickhead!'

'What dickhead say when we crash into that car?'

'If we crashed into that car, the person would probably say, *Ouch*.'

(A truck whizzes past us, sucking us towards it, coating the windscreen in a mist of spray.)

'When we crash into that truck we will go to hospital?'

'This conversation must now stop,' Nicholas declares.

In the morning I fly back to Adelaide and catch a taxi to the hospice.

'I was hoping it was you,' says my aunt, opening the door of Moggy's room. 'Look who's come to see you, Mother.'

She is tiny under the sheets, aside from the pregnancy of her tumour, but then she opens her brilliant eyes and I recognise my grandmother. *Cat's eyes*, her sister-in-law called them, and named her Moggy.

'Darling girl,' she rasps. 'How's that boy?'

'Wonderful.'

'I'm sorry I have no voice.'

'My boy lost his voice on the weekend too. It delighted him, because he sounded like a pirate.'

Her parched mouth widens a little. 'What a boy.'

I place half a teaspoon of ice in her mouth, and she closes her eyes. 'Talk to me, dear.'

What is there to talk about? She worries that my work makes me too busy, so I talk about you instead. Even when she seems to doze off, I keep talking. I am tired of being away from you. You are planning your third birthday party, even though it is five months away. Each guest must bring a lion toy. You have requested pirate candles and party hats and a *very cold* cake.

When the oncologist comes in, Moggy struggles awake to act as hostess. 'Are you the doctor who knows my grand-daughter?'

'No, but I can certainly see the resemblance.'

'I'm flattered,' Moggy rasps.

'No, Mog. I'm the one who's flattered.'

She has always been striking, but there is something rarefied about her now. Her face is smooth as a child's against the white linen; her arms are long and austere, the fine skin falling from the bones like parachute silk.

'Are you feeling any pain?' asks the doctor.

I squeeze her hand, willing her to say yes so that they increase her morphine.

'Only discomfort.'

'Are you feeling worried?'

'Oh no. I finished my worries yesterday.'

She half-smiles and closes her eyes again. This gradual divestment. Last week she finished eating and drinking. Yesterday she finished worrying. So that the only things that remain are breathing, and loving.

My aunt brings Bob into the room. He stumbles over to the bed, weeping: 'I'm still here for you, love.'

I leave them alone and get a coffee, and when I return, she is asleep.

'It's been a good day,' says Nicholas that night, on the computer. 'But the boy's got a few thorny questions.'

You lean into the camera. 'What does die mean, Mama?'

'It means come to the end of your life.'

'What is life?'

'Over to you,' Nicholas laughs.

'It's a bit tricky to explain. Life is when you begin as a baby, and then become a boy, and then a man and then an old man. And then you get to the end of it. You finish being yourself.'

'What I going to be next when I finish being myself?'

'I don't know.'

'Is it a bit like going away and never coming back?'

'Exactly.'

'But where you gone?'

'I don't know.'

You lean in further to the screen, so that all I can see are your huge grave eyes, focusing somewhere to the left.

'I think you go out to sea,' you decide.

On the second day, Moggy can no longer talk and is mostly asleep. She wakes when I arrive and reaches out both of her hands to grasp mine. They surprise me with their warmth, with their strength, and as I hold them, I recognise my own hands in fifty years' time, and wonder if the doctor was right about our resemblance. I sit at her bedside with Baba, and wait. Every time her breath stops, we hold our breaths too, hoping this might be the last time, but then the breath starts again and she continues with her life. It is the opposite of those sleepless nights with you, checking the green light of your sensor. How little I used to trust your breath. Now, as we wait for Moggy to stop breathing for the first time in eighty-eight years, I see how powerful the breath is. How relentless a machine.

On the wall opposite there is a photo of Grandpa, propped up under the clock. *Is a grandpa a type of big thing?* He sits regally in an armchair in the sunroom of their old house; the afternoon sun falls in a square patch on his maroon cardigan. As I listen to Moggy's laboured breath, I remember a dinner years ago, before you were born, when I was still a child. The grown-ups were in the kitchen, preparing dessert, and I found myself alone in the dining room with Grandpa. He was explaining some intricacy of genetic throwback, and I was doing my best to understand, to pretend I understood, but I could smell the sweetness of the baked pineapple: surely it was ready by now, surely they would be returning soon. *The long and the short of it is that at any given time, any child can bear a striking resemblance to an ancestor of several generations back.* Baba had hung photographs of our ancestors in the front passage. Dour-looking people in uncomfortable clothes, in sepia and black and white. I did not especially want them to return.

Then when you were born, so big and ruddy and with that great dome of a head, Baba sent me a photo. It was Grandpa as a baby, cavorting in a giant seashell, with dimpled elbows and fat knees. I had never known him so frivolous. But it was also you, transported back in time to 1918. As bonny, as succulent, as bursting with life as you are now.

The following day, Moggy's mouth has collapsed to one side, and the pauses between her breaths have become longer. My two aunts come in to join Baba, and I move to the armchair by the window, surrendering the bedside to her daughters. Lit by the salt lamp, each of their faces wears a different expression: bewilderment, concern, resignation.

'Do you think she wants more eye drops?'

'Let the poor darling sleep.'

It is like waiting for the moment of a birth. But it is a quieter waiting, aside from her strained breath. The oncologist returns. 'You have to labour to leave this world,' she explains, 'just as you have to labour to enter it.'

Later, my uncle arrives, and then Sash comes to collect me. She wraps her arm around me on the way to the car. 'How are you feeling?'

'If I keep on eating, I'm better. What about you?'

'Okay, considering. Cultivating denial.'

We arrive at a different hospital, where we sit down in the waiting room, and pick up magazines but do not read them.

'You know she's given me the hydrangeas,' she says.

'It's a great responsibility.'

'Tell me about it. Baba's been calling every day. *You know why they're called hydrangeas? Because they need lots of water.*'

We both laugh.

'A great big sob would help,' she says, 'but it just hasn't happened yet.'

The sonographer calls us in, and I lie down on the bed and lift up my top. She rubs gel on my abdomen and applies the cool transducer. A little bit of probing, and then here we are again.

Life's relentless beat, at 146 flashes per minute.

I told Moggy the news three days ago, when she could still talk.

'Ooh!' she gasped. 'Wouldn't it be lovely for you to have a girl!'

Now, as we wait for the images, I text the rest of the family. *All good. Seven weeks pregnant.*

Baba replies with an uncharacteristic spelling error: *Grear*. And then immediately afterwards: *Moggy just died.*

Sometimes the universe is this heavy-handed with its mathematics, after all. As Sash drives us back to the hospice, I clasp these new images tightly. What is life? It might be tricky to explain, but you know when you are right in the middle of it. Moggy's still-warm forehead, as we kiss it for a final time. And inside me your new brother or sister, still just a rhythm. Yet to acquire a voice, or worries, or breath, or love.

*

Several weeks after the funeral, we tell you about the new baby. At first you are silent, and then you furrow your forehead in that way I adore, with the ostentatious seriousness of a news anchor.

'Who is it?'

'We don't know yet.'

'What the baby will say when I say *hocus pocus*?'

'I think the baby would probably laugh.'

You jump off the sofa and ride your tricycle very fast down the hallway.

'Can that be all?' asks Nicholas.

But the following morning you wake armed with questions. Overnight you seem to have intuited the danger. 'Will the baby not fall out of your belly-button?'

'No. My belly-button is too small.'

'What I will say if the baby touch the power point?'

'You'll say *no! Stop!* And then you'll come and get me.'

'What I will say if the baby eat some donkey poo?'

'I don't think you need to worry about that. We hardly ever come across donkey poo.'

'But what I will say when we do?'

It seems your hyper-vigilance might rival mine. 'You'd tell the baby to spit it out, and then you'd come and tell me.'

You scramble up on to my lap, and huddle into my chest. 'Will the baby not scare me?' you whisper.

'Not a big boy like you. The baby's only little, and you're going to be its big brother.'

You turn around to face me, so that I can watch the thoughts flicker across your face, rehearsals for your future life as big brother, when this is your life to share. All of a sudden you look very pleased. 'I want to show the baby a pirate ship.'

'Will the baby be scared?'

'No, Mummy! The baby will be happy.'

ACKNOWLEDGEMENTS

Enormous thanks to my publisher Chris Feik, for seeing the bones of this book before I could, and to the magnificent team at Black Inc., especially Nikola Lusk, Sophy Williams, Peter Long and Elisabeth Young. Thanks also to my dear friend and agent Clare Forster, for support, guidance and pirate sleepovers.

I am grateful to Varuna Writers' House for providing such an amenable venue in which to begin this project; to Janet Clarke Hall at the University of Melbourne, my second home; and to the J.M. Coetzee Centre for Creative Practice at the University of Adelaide.

A version of 'Sleep' previously appeared in the *Monthly*, with the title 'Comforter'.

Thank you to the members of my family for helping raise my children, for allowing themselves to be written about, and for then having the grace to provide editorial feedback: Helen Goldsworthy, Peter Goldsworthy, Daniel and Mary-Anne Goldsworthy, Alexandra Goldsworthy, Mary Dowling, and the late Molly

Wharldall. Equal thanks to other members of my family, spared mention for reasons of space, who have played large roles offstage, particularly Alberta Dowling, Alexandra Hooper, Peter Backhouse, Lisa Temple, Imran Ali, and Jan and Reuben Goldsworthy. Thank you to Eleonora Sivan, for the musical playlists, and for all the lessons in language.

I have drawn limitless succour and inspiration from my gang of mothers: Jade Maitre, Helen Ayres, Angela Maguire, Josephine Vains, Anne-Catherine Lethbridge, Liz Agostino, Sophie Dunstone and Katrina Germein.

Biggest thanks (or apologies) to my sons, Reuben and Otto, and to Nicholas Purcell, co-pilot and collaborator, in this and all else.